My Senior Year
A Guide for
High School Seniors and Their Parents

Daniel A. Reed

My Senior Year
A Guide For High School Seniors and Their Parents

Copyright © 2015 Daniel A. Reed

First Printing
Printed in the United States of America

Published by
Darcon Publishing
Glenville, West Virginia

Edited by Ann M. Reed

ISBN: 0983193916
ISBN-13: 978-0983193913
Library of Congress Control Number: 2015909113

ACT® is a registered trademark of ACT, Inc.
CLEP® is a registered trademark of the College Board, Inc
Fastweb® is a registered trademark of Fastweb, Inc.
FAFSA® is a registered trademark of the U.S. Department of Education
GED® is a registered trademark of the American Council on Education
Google® is a registered trademark of Google, Inc.
NCAA® is a registered trademark of the National College Athletic Association
SAT® is a registered trademark of The College Board, Inc.
TASC® is a registered trademark of CTB/McGraw-Hill, Inc.

The use of any trademarked product names are for educational purposes only.

DISCLAIMER: This book is intended to be used as a guide and should be utilized with appropriate guidance from qualified individuals such as school counselors and other educational professionals. It should not be considered a substitute for any guidance they are able to provide. The author and publisher have made every effort in the preparation of this book to ensure the accuracy of the information contained herein. However, the information in this book is sold without warranty, either expressed or implied. Neither the author nor the publisher will be liable for any damages or losses caused or alleged to be caused, directly, indirectly, incidentally, or consequentially by the information in this book.

Discounts for bulk sales are available. Please contact Sales@DanielAReed.com for more information.

Dedicated to my father and mother.

Alvin S. Reed 1936-2001
Peggy J. Reed 1937-2007

CONTENTS

ACKNOWLEDGMENTS

First and foremost, I would like to acknowledge the efforts and patience of my wife, Ann, who assisted with this project in so many ways.

I would also like to acknowledge all the students that I have had the pleasure of working with over the years. You have kept me young at heart.

Introduction

So here you are. You have gone through all those years of school, and your Senior year has finally arrived. You have memories - some happy, others....well....not so happy. You have had good times and bad. You have taken classes you have liked, and some you haven't. You have teachers you remember, and teachers you would rather forget. Either way, here you are and this is your Senior year. Whether you look forward to your Senior year being over, or if you are saddened because this is your last year of school before moving on to college, the military, trade school, a job - whatever the future holds, this is it. What you decide to do now can help you achieve your future goals, or it can make your future a lot more complicated. You can use this year to actively prepare for your future, or you can let the year slip by and simply hope that your future turns out well.

Because you are reading this, we are going to go with the assumption that you want to do everything in your power to make the most of your Senior year. Our goal is to help you develop a game plan so that you can make sure you have all your "bases covered and your ducks in a row."

"How are you going to do that," you ask? Good question. The plan is to lay out the tasks of your Senior year on a monthly basis and to give you simple insights related to the tasks you need to be thinking about and doing each month. We are going to break things down into easy and doable steps. Additionally, we are going to give you some real stories from recent graduates so that you can see how they dealt with the various issues they encountered over the course of their Senior year. Hopefully it will become clear to you that everyone else survived their Senior year, and so will you.

Well then! Let's get started. It is your Senior year. Don't forget to have some fun along the way!

How To Use This Book

When you first get this book, it is suggested that you read it completely through in its entirety. That's right. All the way through. Don't skip through sections or not read a section because you think that it doesn't apply to you. Why? Because you need to get an idea of the overall timeline of the sequence of events as they unfold during your Senior year. Don't worry about trying to remember everything you need to accomplish the first time you read things through. Simply read the book and let the information ooze into your brain, and then relax.

By reading through everything first, not only will you begin to have an understanding about what you should expect and approximately when you should expect it, you may also be likely to come across some information of which you had not previously been aware. Perhaps you didn't know that you could take the ACT multiple times, or maybe you didn't think about the fact that if one of your parents was in the military you might have most of the cost of your schooling already paid.

Read the book through. Then, talk to your parents and your school counselor about some of the ideas you have as a result of your reading. Most importantly, DON'T STRESS! It is easy to get overwhelmed when you think about the "big picture." Keep in mind that we are going to break things down into small chunks and give you plenty of time to consider what you need to do in order to accomplish your post-secondary (after high school) goals.

After you have read through the book once, put it aside for a while. Let your brain "stew" on the new information you have read. By, "a while," we don't mean two or three weeks. Instead, we're talking about two or three days. Consider your options. Talk to people. Ask questions. The point of this book is to help you develop ideas, plans, and strategies. It also serves as a map to help you navigate the issues and topics you may encounter during your Senior year. Finally it provides you with an idea about the things you need to be discussing with your parents and your school counselor throughout the year. Use the tools in this book to build your future, but don't forget to ask for help along the way.

After you have given your situation some consideration and have talked with the appropriate people in your life, start at the beginning of the book again and pick out the things you need to be doing immediately and that apply to you. Take things a month at a time, and don't overwhelm yourself. Feel free to underline items in the book, write notes in the margins, turn down the pages, highlight sections – do whatever you need to do to make the process of understanding your Senior year activities easier. At the end of each month we have included a page for you to make notes or leave reminders for yourself. Use that space to write down phone numbers, addresses, or other contact information for schools or individuals who can help you. It's your book. Use it however you need to in order to get the most out of it.

Tip!

If you don't know what the symbol above is, it is called a Quick Response (QR) code. With a device such as a smart phone or a tablet, you can download an app that lets you scan the image, and it will automatically take you to the website we have referenced.

Read the book, talk to your counselor, and make your plan. Your counselor may have suggestions of other things you need to be doing each month, so make sure you talk to them about their thoughts and ideas as well. Use the book as a guide to help to keep you on track.

ISSUE ALERT!

Keep in mind that this book is a **GUIDE** not a **PLAN.** It is not meant to replace the expertise that your school counselor has to help you develop a plan for your future. Do not rely on this book without consulting with the appropriate people in your high school. While this book can help guide you, make sure you consult with your school counselor to develop a plan.

Things To Ponder

Graduation Countdown: Your First Day Back

Summer is over, and as you wander in to the school for the first time as a Senior, you may be feeling any number of things. Some people feel like they can conquer the world. Others feel sick. Some have "Senior-itis" (defined as the decreased motivation of Seniors nearing the end of high school) from the first day. Still others feel a combination of emotions that they can't really describe. You may also be one of those people who really doesn't feel any differently than they ever have any other year.

The point is that EVERYONE feels differently. EVERYONE has a different perspective on their Senior year. These differences of perspective can actually be quite irritating after a while, especially when classmates talk about them all the time. Over the next few days, weeks, or months, you may become aggravated with your classmates because they, "can't wait to get out of here," or you may get annoyed with them because they are so, "stuck in high school." You may be ready to leave and "get away from the drama." The possibility exists that you see yourself as different from everyone else, and you might feel like no one understands how you see your life right now. Believe it or not, all these feelings can happen on your first day back at school. Or….they might not. How people deal with these issues, yourself included, is wholly dependent on individual levels of coping skills. To some people, this change means nothing. To others, it means a great deal.

Why is this something you should know about? These expressed differences of perspective and attitudes can have detrimental effects on the relationships between you and your classmates. You need to prepare for the potential stress related to the changes in your relationships. People who have been very close through many years of school together might suddenly find themselves exceptionally irritated with their friend's behaviors. Everyone handles stress differently, and how your friends are acting is a result of how they are coping with the impending change that is coming at graduation.

Rarely has a year gone by where at some point during the year the members of the Senior class start getting irritated with each other; some to the point of hating each other. Does this *always* happen every year? No. But, it does happen frequently. Every year students are in the counselor's office venting about how they are so irritated with another student because, "they just want to get out of here, and that is all they talk about," or they say, "I can't stand so-and-so anymore because they are so juvenile. It's like they can't grow up and let go."

So, again; why are we pointing this out to you? You need to know that these situations happen, and that they happen more frequently than you would imagine. If you are aware of this phenomenon, you can begin to notice when it starts to happen to you or the people around you. Being aware of this one little fact can help ease some of the emotional turmoil that can accompany being a Senior.

Be respectful of other people's perspectives. When you find yourself starting to get irritated with your classmates, acknowledge that they are dealing with the idea of change. They may be scared and are trying to put on a brave front. They may be elated and want to share their happiness that they have finally made it to their Senior year. If you find yourself getting irritated with others, ask yourself, "Why is their attitude bothering me so much?" Perhaps your reaction is because you are not coping well with the change and maybe you are overly sensitive right now.

Your relationships are going to change and that's okay. It is part of growing up. Be aware of the changes, and try to be understanding of other people's differences of opinion. You will be glad you did, for your own peace of mind.

OK....First Day Back! What Should I Do?

What should you do on your first day back in school to begin preparations for your future? There is one very important thing you need to do, and you need to take it quite seriously. Here it is:

RELAX....

That's right. Chill out. Relax. "Chillax." Enjoy being back with your friends. You have the whole year to get things done. You don't need to worry about scholarship applications today or what school you will be attending, or what job you will have when you graduate. For today, simply relax. Besides, you probably won't be able to get much help from anyone today anyway. School counselors and administrators are going to be tied up with the details of getting the school year off to a proper start. They will be doing things like changing schedules, taking care of getting teacher's rosters, enrolling new students, and so on. If you are one of those people who needs a schedule change, then by all means, go see your counselor. But, don't worry about asking for scholarship information and such things right now. Just go to class, enjoy your day, and settle in to your routine.

But When Do I Need To Start Worrying About What I Need To Be Doing?!?!

Believe it or not, it takes a couple of weeks for counselors and administrators to get things in order at the beginning of the school year. Give them some time to get their beginning of year tasks completed. Once they get settled in to their routine then you can start talking to them about your plans. Waiting two or three weeks into the school year is usually good. Of course, all of this depends on the size of your school, how many counselors you have, and what the counselor's duties entail.

Generally, when a counselor is ready to start working with students to help them with scholarship applications, résumés, plans for the future, etc., they will let you know. If they don't, then you are going to have to go to them and get the ball rolling. A good rule of thumb is that if you haven't heard from your counselor within two or three weeks after the beginning of the school year, then you need to go to them.

Hopefully you have a good school counselor who is interested in helping you, and has the job that they do because they like helping students. But, think about this: Lots of people have driver's licenses. Does having a driver's license automatically make someone a good driver? No. Similarly, just because a person has all the degrees and certifications to be a counselor doesn't necessarily make them a good counselor. Let's face it, you may have a dud. You may need to seek them out to get information. Not every counselor makes themselves easily accessible. If you have a counselor that you never see, make it a point to go see them. Let them know who you are and what you are interested in doing in the future. Ask them questions. Find out how they get information to the students. Don't be afraid to approach them, because it is their job to help you.

Having said that, being a school counselor isn't easy. Even the good ones get a bad rap from time to time. They have lots of things for which they are responsible and students or teachers aren't always aware of what counselors do. Additionally, your school counselor may be trying to keep track of hundreds of different students at your school and they may barely know who you are. If this is the case, it is your job to get to know them.

Every year there are Seniors who practically "live" in the counselor's office. They are constantly filling out college applications, doing scholarship applications and talking about their future. Conversely, there are students who never darken the door of the counselor's office over the course of the year, and who just want to be left alone. If you think you are one of those students who can take care of everything on your own, that's fine. But, don't be one of those students who never goes to see the counselor or ask them any questions, and yet complains that no one is there to help you. Ask for help. Get to know your counselor. You might actually like them!

What Are My Options?

There are many choices as to what you can do after graduating high school. The important thing is that you do SOMETHING. What are your options? Let's examine some of them.

Lots of people have it in their mind that going to college is the obvious next step after graduating high school. But let's face it: College isn't right for everyone. You can be quite successful without going to college. While it is true that your earning potential increases with the more education you have, the key to success isn't always about how much money you make annually. You have to enjoy what you do. Nothing is worse than going to work every day and hating your job. Make sure that you enjoy the field you choose to enter, and don't choose a to study something or take a job simply because other people want you to.

A few things for you to consider:

1.) *Don't* choose to go in to a field just because you have a friend who thinks it would be good for you.

2.) *Don't* plan on going to a college or university just because your current girlfriend or boyfriend is attending that school.

3.) *Do* pick a field of study or a career path because it interests *you*, not your friends or your parents.

Some parents may not like to hear that they shouldn't force their child into a certain career path. But if a parent truly wants what is best for their child, they need to consider the child's happiness 20 years in the future as a factor in that child's wellbeing today. Just because they think their child will be successful in a field and that they "should" go in to it, doesn't make it so. Guide your children, but don't force them down a path. You, and they, will be happier in the long run.

Basically after high school you have the following options from which to choose:

- Go to college
- Go to a vocational/technical/proprietary school
- Go into the military

- Get a job
- Be a bum

Realize of course, you can combine either of the first three options with either of the second two options as well. There have been quite a few bums enrolled in schools over the years. These were people who were in school just to get a financial aid check, and also included student loans. Sometimes these people take the money and run, defaulting on student loans, and then go on to leach money from some other source. Don't be one of these people.

Let's look at each of these options and try to determine which of them may be best for you (except the option of being a bum…people who fall in to that category probably aren't reading this anyway….)

Going To College

Do you plan on being a doctor, lawyer, teacher, engineer, professor, researcher, chemist, biologist, mathematician, accountant, statistician, financial analyst, geologist, (and the list goes on, and on, and on)? Then you need a college degree. There are different types of college degrees. Some examples are:

- An Associate Degree (A.S, or A.A)
- A Bachelor's Degree (B.S. or B.A)
- An Educational Specialist Degree (Ed.S)

- A Master's Degree (M.S. or M.A.)
- A Doctoral Degree (Ph.D, Ed.D., PsyD., etc.)
- A Professional Degree (J.D., M.D., D.O, etc.)

Let's look at each one of these degrees in a little more detail.

Associate Degree

An Associate Degree is a two year degree that is awarded by community colleges, junior colleges, technical colleges, and some four-year colleges and universities. Various schools have different requirements, but generally an Associate Degree requires a minimum of 60 credits to complete, with each class you take being worth X number of credits. For example, one class may be worth 3 credits, and another class may be worth 2 credits. You would take the number of required classes to complete a total of 60 credit hours.

There are usually two different types of Associates degrees; one is an *Associate of Arts,* and the other is *Associate of Science.* What's the difference?

An Associate of Arts degree usually requires you take a set of basic classes for general education purposes (Math, English, Social Studies) plus additional classes in areas such as English, Literature, Social Science, and so on. An Associate of Science degree usually requires a set of basic classes for general education (again, Math, English, and Social Studies) but requires additional classes in areas such as Math and/or Science.

While it is often referred to as a "two-year" degree, it is possible to finish an associate degree prior to two years, or it can take much longer than that. A variety of factors may prolong or shorten the completion time. This holds true for any degree.

Bachelor's Degree

A Bachelor's Degree is a four year degree that is awarded by four year colleges and universities. There are generally two different types of Bachelor degrees, as there was with the Associate Degree. One is a *Bachelor of Science* and the other is a *Bachelor of Arts.* The primary difference between the two types of degrees is the number of classes required in Humanities based courses (English, Literature, Social Science, etc.) or Math and/or Science based courses. If a degree requires more Humanities courses, it is most likely a Bachelor of Arts Degree. If the degree requires more Math and/or Science courses, it is most likely a Bachelor of Science Degree.

Master's Degree

A Master's Degree is an advanced degree beyond a Bachelor's Degree. People who have a Master's Degree have demonstrated that they have a high level of understanding in a specific area of study. As with the other degrees, there are Master of Arts degrees, which have more humanities based classes, and Masters of Science degrees in which the student has to take more science and/or math based classes. It usually takes 2 to 4 years of study beyond a Bachelor's Degree to get this degree.

Educational Specialist

An Educational Specialist degree is a terminal degree (the last degree you can have in a field of study) beyond a Master's degree. It is for people who wish to develop an advanced knowledge of a subject, but do not want or need to complete a doctoral degree. It usually takes 2 to 3 years of study beyond a Master's degree to get this degree.

Doctoral Degree

A Doctoral Degree is the highest degree you can obtain in any field of study. It is awarded by universities and usually requires 4 to 7 years of study beyond a Master's degree. Doctoral Degrees can be obtained in any field of study. Contrary to what some people might think, someone can be considered a doctor and not have any medical training. There are different types of Doctoral Degrees, such as a Phd., an EdD., an PsyD, etc., and all have different requirements for completion.

Professional Degree

Professional degrees are awarded to those people who complete programs of study in law, medicine, pharmacy, etc. Depending on the degree it may take 3 to 4 years beyond a Bachelor's degree or perhaps as many as 8 to 10 years.

Some students are often surprised to find out that in order to do the job they want, they have to get more of an education than they originally anticipated. Make sure you talk to your counselor and research what level of education and training it takes to do the job you want.

Vocational/Technical/Proprietary Schools

Vocational/Technical schools are for those individuals who want further training in a specific skillset. Some high schools may offer vocational or technical training as part of their school curriculum, but there are always other opportunities beyond high school to further your training in any given field. To that end, a student might want to consider obtaining more training in order to become more marketable in the field in which they plan to get a job.

Some vocational or trade schools are standalone institutions, in that they are like a private training facility akin to a private college or university. Other types of vocational or trade schools may actually be associated with colleges and universities and students who attend these schools may end up having to take a few basic college classes. For example, a student at such a school may need to take English or Math classes along with their actual vocational or technical classes in order to earn the certification they desire.

Some colleges that offer vocational/technical training may actually award a type of Associate Degree called an Applied Associate of Science, or A.A.S.. An A.A.S. Degree can be conferred in a number of fields, including welding, criminal justice, hospitality services, as well as others. There are any number of possibilities available for students to explore.

There are many reasons some people want to continue with vocational or technical training after they graduate high school. First, it doesn't take as long to complete a certificate program as it does to complete a two or four year college degree. Because it doesn't take as long, students can get into the workforce faster than they would if they went to college. Secondly, it gives students who complete the training an advantage over students who simply have a high school diploma. If an employer has two candidates for a job and one of those candidates has advanced training, it would most likely be in that employer's best interest to hire the individual with the most training over the one who only has a high school diploma. You might think it is a pain to keep going to school after you graduate high school, but doing so can have huge benefits in the long run.

If you are interested in pursuing a vocational/technical certification or degree after you graduate high school, check with your school counselor to see what options are available for you. The counselor can provide you with ideas about what schools are available for you to continue your training, as well as perhaps give you some other ideas worth considering.

Another type of school which falls into the vocational/technical category is called a proprietary school. These are schools that teach a trade or vocation, but instead of being associated with a university or college they are privately owned by an individual or corporation. An example of this may be a beauty school, or a neuromuscular massage therapy school. As another example, some fast food restaurant chains have training facilities wherein they offer classes for their employees to become managers. When an employee finishes these programs of study (usually two or three weeks long), they are awarded a certificate of completion by the corporation. These types of facilities are all considered proprietary schools because they are privately owned.

If you are looking at a proprietary school as an option for continued training after you graduate high school, keep in mind that not all of these schools are qualified by the Department of Education to be eligible for federal financial aid. You may have to pay for the training you receive from them out of your own pocket. Some scholarships may be available for this type of training, but often the availability will be limited.

Another thing you need to consider is that any credits that you earn at proprietary schools are most likely going to be non-transferable to another institution unless the accepting institution has a program in place that allows for such transfers. Again, check with your counselor, as they will most likely have the information you need about what schools are available to you and what they offer.

Military Service

If you are interested in joining the armed services, you need to start considering what branch of the military you want to join. You will need to think about scheduling appointments with military recruiters, and meeting with them throughout the year to discuss your options and your progress in school. The school counselor will generally know when recruiters from the various branches of the military are coming to your school. Check with your counselor about potentially meeting with recruiters if you are interested.

One last thing you need to consider when talking to the military: Don't limit yourself to talking to recruiters from just one branch of the military. By taking the time to talk to recruiters from all of the various military branches, you open yourself up to more possibilities. Keep in mind that it never hurts to talk, and that you are not committed to any type of service until you sign your enlistment papers.

ISSUE ALERT!

One thing that most students are unaware of is the fact that high schools are required by law to share your name, address, and telephone number with military recruiters. Don't be surprised if you get a call from a military recruiter even though you haven't expressed any interest in joining the military.

Military service educational benefits are an option for students who wish to go to school after high school but feel they cannot afford to do so. The military offers a number of options to assist you in paying for school. For example, the **Armed Services Tuition Assistance Program** allows for both enlisted individuals and officers in the military to receive up to $4,500 annually to fund tuition and fees at a college or university.

Before you decide to run out and enlist, you need to be aware that there are some restrictions that apply. Eligibility for these funds, along with requirements related to your years of service, the type of service you will provide, and a variety of other variables, are different with each branch of the military. Also, the application process for acquiring these funds is different for each of the various branches as well. Things are even more involved if you enter the National Guard or the Reserves.

Another option for using the military to pay for continuing your education is the **Post-9/11 GI Bill**. This particular benefit is offered to members of the military who have served at least 90 days on active duty since September 11, 2001. Depending on how long you serve, the bill will pay between 40% to 100% of your tuition and fees at an in-state (the state where you live) public college or university, or up to $17,500 at a private or foreign school.

Another benefit of military service is called the **Montgomery GI Bill**. With this particular type of assistance, military service members are required to pay $100 a month for a year (totaling $1200) in order to receive a monthly educational benefit. The amount that you can receive varies, but it is possible that a full time college student could receive up to $1,500 a month.

Finally, there is the option of Reserve Officers' Training Corps, or the **ROTC** for short. By enrolling in an ROTC program, you receive training to develop leadership skills that prepares you to enter the armed services once you graduate college. Some students in ROTC programs actually have their college education paid for in full by the program. Additionally, when some ROTC students graduate from college they are commissioned as officers in the military upon graduation.

There are many things you need to consider when thinking about enlisting in the military as a means of paying for college. Enlisting isn't something that should be taken lightly or that you should rush into without thinking about it long and hard. Let's look at some of the pros and cons of military service, and explore them more fully.

One of the biggest advantages for you to consider about military service is that most, if not all, of your tuition and fees can be paid for by the military. Obviously, this can be a very good thing, especially if you have limited resources.

Another advantage of military service as it relates to your education is that some of your training in the military may translate into college credit, i.e., the leadership courses you might take, for example. Given the foregoing, training received in the military can shorten the amount of time you are in college, though probably not by much. Many of the classes you would receive credit for in the military will most likely be considered elective courses at a college or university, and as such would not necessarily apply directly toward your degree. Once you have served your time in the military, you will need to check with an advisor at the particular college you are interested in attending to see how (or if) your service training will translate into college credit.

If you join the military, your children may also reap the benefits of your service. Depending on the circumstances, the new Post 9/11 GI Bill allows for the transfer of your educational benefits to either your spouse or your children. You also need to be aware of that as of October 2011, the benefits you obtain from the GI Bill can also be used for non-degree programs and other training, such as culinary school, welding programs, and so on. This is a wonderful option if you are wanting to pursue something other than a traditional college education.

Tip! If you have a parent who served in the military, you need to check to see if they have any military benefits that would help you pay for school.

When thinking about all the positive aspects of using military benefits to help pay for continuing your education, you also need to consider potential drawbacks. Let's look at some of the possible issues of which you need to be aware.

Imagine you are mid semester in college, and suddenly you get word that you are going to be deployed into active duty, effective immediately. This is a very real possibility. The good news is that schools are required to work with students who are in the military to ensure that being deployed doesn't negatively affect their schooling. In order to do this however, you will most likely need to withdraw from school for an undetermined amount of time. While your time in active service will not be held against you toward the completion of your degree, you most likely will not be able to simply start back in the individual classes you were enrolled in at the point where you left off when you were deployed. Once your deployment time is over, you can re-enroll, but you will need to start your classes that you withdrew from over again from the beginning. Individual school policies vary, so you will need to check with the school to find out how they handle this issue.

Another thing you need to consider when joining the military is that you may also be relocated from time to time, which can also cause delays in your academic progress. This can be a problem in that classes that are required at one school for a specific degree may not transfer to another school as a graduation requirement for the same degree. Schools tend to work with military service personnel as much as they can within the parameters of their institutional policies in order to facilitate transfer credit, but you may end up with a number of electives by the time you are finished with your degree that you don't really need.

Another major issues people encounter with military tuition benefits is that they expire. Make sure that you use your benefits within the specified date ranges and submit all the appropriate paperwork accordingly, or all the effort you put in to obtaining the benefits may be for nothing.

Getting A Job

If you don't want to go to school anymore after you graduate, and you don't want to go into the military, you need to think about getting a job. One of the biggest delusions that some students labor under is that they are going to graduate from high school and instantly start making upwards of $50,000 a year. While this is not entirely out of the realm of possibility, it simply isn't likely that this will be your reality. Think of it this way: If you roll six dice simultaneously it is possible that you could roll all sixes on the first roll, but it isn't very likely. Your odds of getting a high dollar job immediately after graduating high school are about the same as rolling all sixes on the first roll of the dice. We're not telling you this to discourage you, but to simply keep you grounded in reality.

If you are considering going straight into a job after high school, you need to start making your plans accordingly. If you are unprepared, you are going to end up struggling. Make good choices now, and your future struggles won't be as difficult.

But I Don't Know What I Want To Do!

If you don't have any idea what you want to do after you graduate, you are not alone. Start asking around and you are sure to discover some of your friends are likely feeling the same way. On one hand, feeling this way isn't a bad thing. You are still young and you have time to explore your options. On the other hand, you are at the point in your life where you need to start making some plans. Keep in mind that plans can change.

When you don't know what to do, you need to prepare for multiple contingencies. It doesn't hurt to get ready to go to a four year college, even if you have no intention of attending at the present. Who knows? You may change your mind at the last minute. It happens, and when it does, those students who did not prepare are left scrambling around trying to get everything in order.

When thinking about what you want to do after you graduate, think realistically about the lifestyle you want to have. Do you want to live like you live now, or do you want more in life? Would you be okay with having less than you do now? Having the lifestyle you want is directly related to what you should be doing during your Senior year to prepare for that life.

You may not know which direction you want to go, so prepare yourself to go in a multitude of directions. Making preparations now keeps you from being limited in the future. Take care of things during this year, and your future self will thank you for the effort.

OK! This is Good, But How Do I Get Money For School!?!?!

Remember earlier when we said to relax? Ok….you need to do that again. You are going to be walked through the financial aid process step by step. For now, the biggest thing you need to be aware of is that you will have to file the Free Application For Federal Student Aid (FAFSA®) in order to get any financial aid at all. It makes no difference where you go to school, you will need to file a FAFSA®.

You cannot file the FAFSA® until after January 1st of each year. However, even though you don't file the FAFSA® until after the first of the year, there are various scholarships you need to be looking for well before then.

Scholarship application deadlines tend to come in waves. Generally, scholarship applications tend to be due in October, January, March and April. While these months are generally when deadlines peak, this doesn't hold true all the time. Whoever set up the scholarship originally, or whoever provides administration for the scholarship, decides the deadlines for application submission. If you want to apply for a scholarship, make sure you keep track of when it is due. We will discuss scholarships and how to find them later in the book.

I'm So Confused. What Do These Words And Acronyms Mean?

Throughout the year, you are going to be hearing a number of terms and acronyms related to your post-secondary life (i.e., life after high school) that you may not understand. Don't worry. If you don't know what a word or acronym means, ask your school counselor. We have also included some of the more common words and acronyms related to your Senior year that you might encounter in the glossary in the back of this book.

The key is not to get frustrated when you get confused and don't understand something. Ask someone who you think would know the answer, and they will help clear up your confusion. If the first person you ask doesn't know the answer, ask someone else. Don't be afraid to ask a teacher or your school counselor. Also, remember that you also have the sum of human knowledge at your fingertips via the internet. You can always look up a meaning of a word or acronym on the web.

So, What Do I Need To Be Doing?

First a word of caution. Thinking about everything you need to be doing over the course of your Senior year can be quite overwhelming. Every year there are always a number of students in the counselor's office in tears (both male and female) who are overwhelmed because they are thinking about everything they need to get done prior to graduating.

So how do you cope? One of the most effective strategies is to deal with problems or tasks as they arise in small chunks. Let's begin by breaking the rest of the year down into months, and talk about various issues you might encounter. Remember, you have lots of people around you to help you along the way. Rely on them, their support and expertise, and you will be in good hands.

Let's get started!

"Your education is the one thing that no one can ever take away from you."

Dr. William K. Simmons

August

At the beginning of the school year, which for the purposes of our discussion we are going to assume to start in August, you need to start thinking about your options. You need to consider what classes you are going to take during your Senior year, though you most likely already took care of your schedule during the final months of your Junior year, or perhaps even over the summer. Having said this, and upon further consideration, you may want to think about some of the following options and talk to you school counselor about how they could possibly fit into your overall plan.

Earning College Credit In High School

Did you know that you can possibly earn college credit, or even test out of certain college classes while you are still in high school? You can, and there are a number of different ways for you to do it. If you are interested in doing this, you need to start early and plan for earning credit by either taking the appropriate classes, taking the right tests, or using a combination of both.

Advanced Placement Classes

One way you can earn credit in college is to take what are referred to as Advanced Placement classes, or "AP classes" for short. These are classes that you take in high school that involve more work than just your average, every-day course. Your school may or may not offer AP courses, so check with your counselor to determine what courses are available.

Once you finish taking an AP course, you will need to sign up to take the AP exam for that course. Your teacher will provide you with information on how to do this. It should be noted that you can take an AP exam without ever having taken an AP class, though doing so isn't recommended. The classes are designed to prepare you for the test. But, theoretically, you can take the test and get college credit simply by scoring the requisite score without ever having had the class.

It does cost a fee to take an AP exam. It only makes sense that you to get your money's worth by adequately preparing for the test.

Whether or not you get AP credit at the college or university you are planning on attending depends on what that institution requires you to score on the AP exam. The scores on the various tests range from 1 to 5, with 1 being the lowest and 5 being the highest. Some colleges may require you to score a minimum of 3 on a specific test in order to award you credit for the class, while others may require you to score a minimum of 4. Some universities even require that you get a 5 in order to be awarded credit at their institution. It all depends on the individual college's policies.

When you talk to the college admissions counselor, or your academic advisor at your new school, make sure that they are aware of the fact that you have taken AP tests, and bring a copy of your scores for them to see. You will need to have the official scores sent directly to the college or university from the company that produces the AP exams, but a copy of the results will suffice for your initial discussions.

Note that just because you receive AP credit at one college or university does not mean that you will receive AP credit for the same classes at another institution if you transfer. These things can be tricky, so make sure you have all the facts.

Dual Credit

Some high schools team up with colleges to offer classes that you take in high school and earn credit for a similar college course simultaneously. For example, you might enroll in an Advanced English 12 class in which you would receive high school credit for English as well as English 101 at a college or university. Most colleges and universities require that you achieve a certain score on an ACT® or SAT® prior to being allowed to take a dual credit course, so check with your counselor for guidelines and restrictions.

Early Entrance Programs

In an early entrance program you actually enroll in a course at a college or university as a high school Senior. For example, some high schools will let you sign out from school and actually go to a nearby college campus during the day to take a course. Or perhaps you may be able to take a course at a college campus or extension office in the evening. Early entrance courses are different from a dual credit classes. With early entrance program classes you are not receiving high school credit for the class, only college credit. Check with your counselor for availability of such opportunities in your area.

The Scoop on Starting College Classes Early

As with most things, there are pros and cons to starting college classes early. An obvious positive point is the fact that you won't have to spend as much time in college.   There are a number of students who have started taking dual credit courses during their junior year in high school, and by the time they entered college they had accumulated enough credits to be considered a sophomore. There are even some students who have had an Associate Degree in college finished when they graduated high school, and earned both degrees simultaneously. Such things are rare, but it can happen.

The down side to taking a large number of classes in high school is that you may have a difficult time finding lower level classes to take once you get into college. Many of the classes you are likely to take as dual credit courses are going to be lower level classes, i.e. 100 or 200 level courses. The only courses remaining for you to take once you get to college could be the more advanced level courses, and they may be difficult for you to enroll in your first year. Given that you need to have a full schedule in order to receive full financial aid benefits, you could end up taking some classes you don't need just to get a full schedule. Also, if you have taken all your basic classes early you may find that you have nothing but upper level classes left to take, and it can be quite taxing on you during your first year or so in college.

> **Tip!** Be sure to do your research and find the suggested plans of study for the program you are interested in pursuing in college. Mapping out what courses you need as well as when they will be offered again can alleviate problems in the future.

I Don't Want To Go To School Anymore...What About Me?

Going on to another school after you graduate high school isn't for everyone. We recognize this reality and don't want to push something on you that you don't want. Having said that, it is important you are aware of some important facts before you make the decision to cease your educational pursuits. Here are some things to consider:

1. The more education that you have, the more money you will earn over the course of your lifetime.

2. Your potential for unemployment goes down the more education you have. The more education

you have the more likely you are to find and keep a job.

Look at the following chart from the Bureau of Labor Statistics. If you are looking to make more money and have and keep a steady job, getting an education past high school is your best bet. Not only that, but the more education you get the more earning potential and employment potential you have.

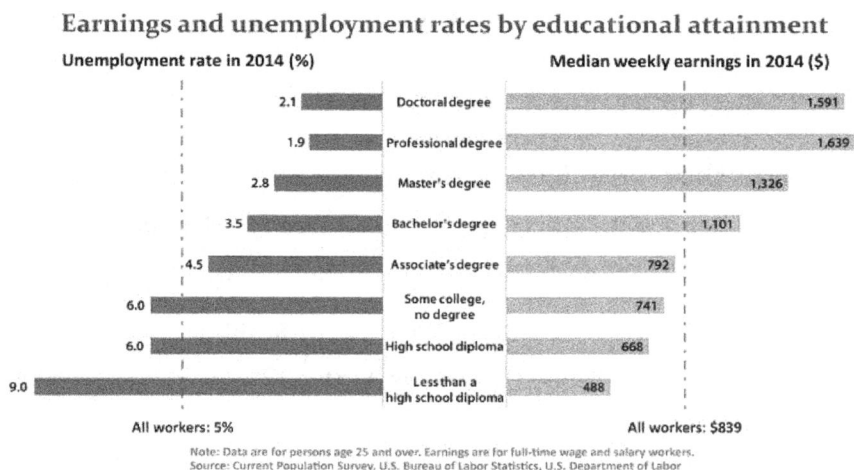

Earnings and unemployment rates by educational attainment

Unemployment rate in 2014 (%)		Median weekly earnings in 2014 ($)
2.1	Doctoral degree	1,591
1.9	Professional degree	1,639
2.8	Master's degree	1,326
3.5	Bachelor's degree	1,101
4.5	Associate's degree	792
6.0	Some college, no degree	741
6.0	High school diploma	668
9.0	Less than a high school diploma	488
All workers: 5%		All workers: $839

Note: Data are for persons age 25 and over. Earnings are for full-time wage and salary workers.
Source: Current Population Survey, U.S. Bureau of Labor Statistics, U.S. Department of Labor

Even after considering these facts, you may still say that you don't want to go on to school and instead want to go to work. If that's the case, you need to think about what jobs you are interested in pursuing once you get out of high school. Think about what you are qualified to do and ask yourself if you think you will be happy doing it. If you can answer, "Yes," to that question, then start looking for and talking to people about potential jobs once you graduate. See what they tell you and make sure to talk to them about what you might need to do to get a job like theirs. You can never start too early creating a network of contacts and making connections with people who work in your field of interest. Perhaps someone you know can facilitate getting you a job with the company or organization where they work. Until you start talking to people in the workforce, you will have a difficult time getting an accurate picture of the employment potential that particular field has to offer.

Find Out Testing Dates for the ACT®/SAT®

Whether you like it or not, if you want to go to college you will have to take a test. However, this doesn't necessarily hold true for you if you want to go to a vocational/technical or proprietary school. So why is it that you have to take these tests at all?

There are a number of reasons schools require you to take the ACT® or SAT®. They are:

1. The tests give colleges a sense of what you already know and on what level you function academically.

2. Because we are a data driven society, the tests provide an overall educational "snapshot" of the students entering college.

3. They are a means of screening people for scholarships. Some scholarships require certain scores on the ACT®/SAT® in order to be eligible for them.

4. The tests provide you the opportunity to test-out of some classes in college. If you score high enough in a subject area, you may not have to take the introductory classes in those areas.

5. The companies that manage the tests offer services which help you to connect to colleges that are a good fit for you by providing your information and scores to schools who might be interested in recruiting you.

There are lots of good resources on the internet to help you study for the tests, and quite a few of them are free. All you need to do is search for "Free ACT®/SAT® Practice Tests," and you will find several.

Some states offer free test preparation guides and practice tests through their State Department of Education web sites. This is something you need to talk to your school counselor about in order to see what resources are available for you.

If you feel like you cannot afford to take the ACT® or SAT®, don't worry. Talk to your counselor about a fee waiver. Both ACT® and SAT® offer fee waivers to schools for their counselors to use to help students who cannot afford to pay for the test.

Tip!

Even if you don't think you are going to college, you should still take the ACT® or SAT®. You would be surprised at the number of people who think they are not going to go to college, and then change their minds at the last minute. At the very least, if you take the test even once it will be one less thing you don't have to worry about making up at the last minute if you do decide to go to college.

The Military Wants You To Take A Test As Well

If you are considering entering the military, you will need to schedule to take the Armed Services Vocational Aptitude Battery ASVAB (AFQT) assessment. You can't enlist without having taken this test. Dates for this test vary, so check with your school counselor to see what opportunities are available in your area if you are interested.

NOTES

"In order to get that little piece of
paper with a pink ribbon tied
around it, you need to have a plan."

Bernard C. McKown

September

Talk To Your Counselor

Sometime during September you need to plan on meeting with your counselor to talk about your plans after graduation. It doesn't make any difference if you plan on going to college, going to a vocational/trade school, or plan on getting a job, you need to talk to your counselor to let them know what you are planning on doing. Counselor's get all kinds of information about scholarships and job opportunities. Talk to them and find out what information they can provide to you.

When you are talking with your counselor, let them know what colleges, universities, technical/vocational schools you are interested in, or for which jobs you are thinking about applying. It is important for your counselor to understand your goals. Keep your options open. Don't make the mistake of not considering a school or a job just because your friends don't like it. Remember, **YOU** are the one who needs to be happy with your choice - not your friends. If you go to a school or take a job just because you want your friends to be happy, you will probably end up being miserable.

ISSUE ALERT!

One of the things that sometimes happens is that some students feel compelled to make fun of their friend's choice of college or of a job. When a so-called "friend" starts making fun of your choice, you need to ask yourself, "Why are they doing this...what is their motivation?"

People who chronically have to find fault with others do so in order to make themselves feel better about their own lives. If they are making fun of your choice, ignore them and keep doing what you feel is in your best interest. Understand that *they* are the ones with something lacking in their lives, even if on the outside it seems that their lives are perfect.

A few other things you need to talk with your counselor about are the dates of important events throughout the year. Ask them for tentative dates of financial aid workshops, college fairs, employment/career fairs, or anything else that might be of benefit to you. Make sure you write the dates for these down so you can prepare for them accordingly. Your counselor may not have an exact date for events at this point, but they should be able to give you an idea of when to expect them.

Stay Organized

Organization is a key element in being successful your Senior year. In addition to all the things you need to keep track of in school normally, (tests, homework, reports, etc.), you now need to keep track of college application deadlines, scholarship application deadlines, and a host of other things.

One of the best ways to keep yourself organized is to use a calendar that allows you to see an entire month at a glance and use it to mark down all the important dates and deadlines of which you want to keep track. If you use a mobile device such as a cell phone or tablet, set reminders for yourself at least a week ahead of when something is due. By setting your reminder at least a week in advance, you will not have something sneak up on you that has a deadline the following day.

In addition to keeping a calendar of important dates, get yourself a three ring binder. Things to keep in this binder would include school applications, scholarship applications,   essays,   resumes,   self-reflection compositions, job applications and everything else you accumulate that relates to your goals after graduation. Keep it organized with all your scholarship applications in one section, all your essays in another section, and perhaps keep copies of your transcripts and test scores in another section. By having your information organized in this fashion it will make finding the item you need much easier, as well as save you time and keep your stress levels down.

In addition to keeping a "hard copy" of your information in a binder, it is recommended that you also keep everything scanned and saved on a thumb drive attached to the binder by a small lanyard. You are less likely to lose your thumb drive if you keep it physically attached to your binder.

Tip!

Don't send anyone anything unless you make a copy of it first. Keep a copy of everything including scholarship applications, essays for scholarships, the Free Application for Federal Student Aid (FAFSA®), letters from schools, and so on. Keep everything in your binder, or scan it and save it to a virtual drive and/or on a thumb drive.

Tip!

It is also a good idea to establish a storage place in the "cloud" on a virtual drive. Google® has free storage and you can save all your documents there and have access to them anywhere you go. It also has the added benefit of never being able to be lost, as you might have happen with a thumb drive or your binder.

Another idea is to email copies of your saved material to yourself. Make sure that you use a clear description in the subject line of your email so you can search for things more easily at a later time.

Here's an example:

To: me@myemailaddress.com

From: me@myemailaddress.com

Subject: Essay for the Windmier Scholarship

It is a good idea to get in the habit of clearly labeling your emails in the subject line. Doing so allows you to check the content of an email at a glance, instead of having to open each one up to read what is in it.

Start Looking For Scholarships Online

The internet is a wonderful tool for finding scholarships. While there are several really good websites that will help you find scholarships for which you are eligible, we recommend using Fastweb®. You can find the website at:

www.fastweb.com

When you use websites such as these they will ask a lot of questions, some of which may make no sense to you. Be patient and answer them accordingly. Each question relates to a potential scholarship. You may be asked what you might find to be a number of "weird" questions, but there are a number of "weird" scholarships in the world. There are scholarships available with all kinds of requirements. For example, are you left-handed? There are scholarships for left-handed people. Do you have red hair? There are scholarships available for that as well. Want to write about how you would react during a Zombie Apocalypse? You could win a scholarship. Seriously, we aren't making this stuff up….there are literally scholarships available for these things, and many more.

ISSUE ALERT!

One word of caution. Some websites are willing to provide you scholarship information if you pay them. Don't use these websites. There are plenty of websites out there which will provide you with exactly the same information for FREE. Some of these fee based websites are very enticing, and guarantee to find you financial aid money, "or your money back." At the very least they will send you a report that says you are eligible for a federal student loan. Given the fact that student loans are considered financial aid, they kept up their end of the bargain, and you got charged for worthless information that you could have found out on your own. Don't pay anyone to look for financial aid for you when you can do just as good of a job as they can for free.

Start Asking About Scholarships and Grants

One of the things you need to start talking to your counselor about are scholarship applications they may receive that won't necessarily appear on national web based scholarship searches. These tend to be "local" scholarships that generally only apply to such a limited group of people, they are rarely made available through any major search engines. Examples of local scholarships would include scholarships that are only for people who graduate from your high school and who are attending a specific local college. Another example could be a group of retired employees from your school district who contribute to a fund for scholarships specifically for graduates from your school system. Local organizations and businesses may also offer scholarships that your counselor may be aware of as well. Sometimes these local scholarships are paid to the student, while other times they are paid directly to the school the student is choosing to attend after graduation. You will never know about any of these local scholarships unless you ask the right people, and in this case the right person for you to ask is your school counselor.

Keep in mind that scholarships are not just for going to college. If you are interested in attending a vocational, technical, or proprietary school, there are also scholarships available for you as well. It is a very common misconception that scholarships and grants are only available to people who are college bound. Don't let this belief keep you from getting money you deserve!

Tip! Check the website of any schools you might be interested in attending, as they usually will have a list of scholarships available for their institution.

Talk To College Recruiters

It is usually sometime in mid to late September that recruiters from various colleges and universities begin making their rounds to visit high schools. Colleges and universities all handle their recruitment processes in a variety of ways. Some have "lunch sessions" where they come during lunch time to meet with potential students, while other institutions may set up individual appointments with students at the high school during the day. Still other colleges may schedule a home visit where recruiters actually come to your home to talk to you. The home visit is usually limited to those students who are "high priority" for the college or university. If a recruiter is willing to come to your home, they are very interested in having you attend their school!

Take time to talk to recruiters about what their respective schools have to offer you. It is a recruiters job to know the facts about their school. Here is a partial list of things you should think about asking them.

- Talk to them about the various programs of study they have at their school. Make sure they have what you want.

- If you are interested in playing a sport, let them know. Ask them about any athletic scholarships that might be available for you.

- Talk to them about what types of student activities they have on their campus.

- Ask them about their graduation rate.

- Do they have job placement services for students once they graduate?

- Ask them about the retention rate of the school, i.e., how many people who start at the school, actually graduate.

- What kind of jobs do students get who graduate from their school, particularly in the program of study in which you are interested?

- Talk to them about what the average class size is at their institution. Do you care if you are one of a hundred other students in a classroom? Or, would you prefer to be in smaller classroom settings?

- Ask the recruiter about campus safety. What types of crimes are common, and where do the majority of those crimes occur?

- Ask about mandatory "quiet times" in the residence halls, along with when the doors are locked, and how the school limits access into the dorms to keep out random people out from off of the street.

- Inquire about laundry services. How are you supposed to keep your sheets and linens clean?

These are things you need to consider when choosing the school that is right for you. You need all the information you can get to make a good decision. The school isn't shy about taking your money to educate you, so don't be shy about asking them lots of questions to decide if you want to go there or not.

Tip!

Keep in mind that it is the college recruiters job to get you to attend their institution. Ask them tough questions and make sure you get an accurate picture of what their institution is like. Some recruiters have a quota of students they are expected to recruit each year, so if you feel like you are being misled by a recruiter, you might want to reconsider attending that particular institution.

Request College Application Information

If you cannot talk to a recruiter personally, (or even if you can), you can generally request application information through the college's website. If you want, give the institution a call. Schools always have people who are willing to chat with you.

Some schools offer you the opportunity to chat with a representative online during specific hours. Others have a "call me now" option, where you enter your phone number onto the website and a representative calls you instantly. Colleges and universities are using all manner of technology to reach out to potential recruits.

Take advantage of how easy they make it for you to talk to them.

Keep in mind that just because you ask an institution for an application doesn't mean that you have to attend that institution. What's more, just because you fill out and submit an application to an institution, doesn't mean you are committed to attend that school. Institutions get any number of applications each year from students who are just "fishing" to see what kind of an offer the college will make to them. To weed out the people who are just curious about the school and who aren't really interested in attending, schools may charge an application fee. The applications are free for you to get, but you may have to pay a fee if you want to actually apply to the institution.

Now is the time you need to start gathering the information you need and getting answers to questions you may have in order to make your decisions later. Don't be afraid! Talk to people! Check out what they have to offer!

Tip!

Be cautious about using any website which offers to assess your interests for free and then automatically signs you up to get information from colleges. By using such a service you may be flooded with telephone calls from schools in which you have no interest in attending. Only contact those schools to which you want to apply directly. Don't have a third party website do it for you.

Go On College/School Visits

One very important, yet often overlooked, component of deciding which school you want to attend is the school visit. You would be amazed at the number of people who decide that they are going to go to a school or college without ever having visited the campus first! Students hear about schools through their friends, TV, or on the internet, and get the idea that it is the perfect school for them. In fact, if they were to visit the school, they could potentially find it isn't at all what they thought it would be.

You cannot form a proper opinion about a place until you have actually been to it. You need to go to the school you would like to attend, take a tour, have a meal in their cafeteria, visit a dorm room, and perhaps sit in on a class in session. A number of people quickly change their minds about a school (either for it or against it) once they actually see the school firsthand.

It is best that you schedule an appointment when you plan on visiting a campus. Many schools require you to have an appointment before they will offer you a tour or provide you with other amenities. Some people simply "show up" at the campus without calling first, and those folks aren't likely to get as much out of the visit as those who call ahead and schedule an appointment.

Many schools will offer you a "free meal" with your tour. Take them up on it. Find out what they have to offer. Eat their food, see if you like it. Some schools have wonderful cafeteria food, while other schools are found to be lacking.

Many schools use college students to give campus tours. If a student gives you a tour, make sure you take the opportunity to talk to them about their classes, what they like about the school, what they dislike, and anything else you can think to ask. Get as much information as you can.

Tip!

Some (if not all) schools that offer dorm rooms have a special room in their residence hall that is set up for students to see when they visit. Schools call this their "model room." This is a marketing tool that they use to show students what "your room could look like!" Keep in mind, this room is a marketing tool. It has been made to look very nice, and usually has a fresh coat of paint on the walls, has all new furniture, nice decorations, a flat screen TV, and all the "bells and whistles" to impress you.

This is not what your room will look like! You will most likely get a bunk bed, a box spring and mattress set, and a desk. Some schools will provide a microwave/refrigerator but not all of them do. You may be expected to purchase your own bedding, and you will definitely have to provide any furniture, decorations, TV's, and so on. If you are shown a "model room" ask to be shown another room that hasn't been decorated. Also, ask about what you will be expected to provide for your room and what the school furnishes.

While you are there, ask the different schools about what scholarships and grants they have available for which you might be able to qualify. Also, ask them what the process is for applying for these grants and scholarships at their school. Some schools will use your application for admission to their school to automatically "enroll" you for their scholarships. Others may require you to fill out a separate scholarship application form. Check with your admissions counselor to determine how their school handles the scholarship application process.

Virtual Tours

Some schools offer a "virtual" tour of their campuses on their school website. If you simply cannot arrange to go to a school in person the virtual tour can be a good, but not a great, alternative.

A virtual tour can also be helpful if you are planning on doing a live visit because it can help you get an idea of the layout of the campus before you visit. It isn't going to give you the same perspective of a school as a real tour will, however. You may get a general idea about a campus, but you definitely won't get the real "feel" unless you have an actual visit.

Tip!

On a virtual tour, the school provides you with the perspective that they want you to see. The images could be edited, the colors brightened, the lawns freshly manicured. A real world tour is the only way you will be able to judge the reality of the imagery they are presenting.

Ask People If They Would Be A Reference Or Write You A Letter

Another thing you need to be doing this time of year is considering who you will ask to provide you letters of references for your various applications. You may not need letters of reference at this very moment, but eventually you will be needing them for scholarships as well as some school applications. Additionally if you are wanting to get a job when you graduate, letters of reference are also a good thing to have at the ready, especially for employers who require them in order to get an interview.

Start early asking people if they would be willing to write you a letter of recommendation or reference. Why would you want to start now, you ask? Good question. The answer is:

Some………..people……….will……be……………..slow……. in………getting…………….you………..their………..letters……..

Did you see how "painful" it was to read that sentence? Imagine having to REALLY wait on someone to get you a letter, especially when you have a deadline looming. It is best to start early and get letters from people because you will have them when you need them. You can use these letters for multiple scholarship applications, as well as school or job applications. Asking early gives people time to get their references completed without making them feel rushed, and it eliminates you being stressed by trying to get them together at the last possible minute.

Tip!

NEVER, EVER put someone down to be a reference for you without asking them first. Not only is asking them the polite thing to do, but it might prevent you from getting a bad reference. You might think that the person you are asking will give you a good reference, but that might not be the case. Also, the person you listed might not be comfortable giving you a reference. Be safe. Ask them first.

Who should you ask for letters? Employers (if you have a job), teachers, counselors, pastors, business owners, almost anyone who knows you well and can vouch for your character can serve as a reference. The only people you shouldn't ask for letters of recommendation are your family members, unless you are otherwise instructed to do so by the application. Generally, scholarship committees and colleges generally don't really care what your family thinks about you, as it is pretty much a given they are going to say nice things about you. So, keep your list of references to people outside your family.

ISSUE ALERT!

Some applications may request that you waive your right to view the references that people provide for you. The theory behind this is that a person who is providing you with a reference is more likely to feel comfortable telling the truth about how they feel about you if they know you are not going to see what they have written.

Compare School Costs

Another thing you need to start doing this month is to begin looking at how much it will cost to attend the schools that you are considering.   The Federal Government has made the process of estimating how much it will cost you to attend a school rather simple. In 2011 the Higher Education Act was amended and it is now required for any postsecondary institution (college, technical school, proprietary school) that receives financial aid money from the government to post a "Net Price Calculator" on their website. Using this calculator will provide you with an **estimate** of the cost of attending that school based on the information you enter. Remember though, nothing is final until you file your FAFSA® and the school has a chance to look at what the government says you need to pay.

The Net Price Calculator is a good place to begin getting an idea of school costs. If a school's website does not have a "Net Price Calculator" on their website, then that school most likely doesn't receive financial aid dollars from the government, and you are most likely going to have to pay for the classes you take out of your own pocket if you attend such a school. If you can't find the calculator at first, don't panic. Some are more difficult to find than others. If you look for it and don't see it, don't be afraid to call the school or send them an email and ask where you might find the Net Price Calculator on their website.

Another tool you can use to get an idea of your financial aid situation would be to visit the FAFSA4CASTER site at www.fafsa.gov. This is a free online calculator that gives you an early estimate of your federal student aid to help you make your plans.

Use the following QR code to go directly to the FAFSA4CASTER website.

If You Haven't Done This Already, Sign Up To Take The ACT®/SAT®

If you have already signed up to take a college entrance test, great! If you haven't, now is when you should consider doing so. If you are a serious, hardcore individual who wants to get the highest possible score you can on these tests, start taking them early because you can take the various tests multiple times. Start now, and you will have plenty of time to work on getting the scores you want. Some people take the tests and score so well on the first attempt that they don't take it again.

Again, if you think that the cost is a factor, talk to your school counselor about getting a fee waiver. Don't let the cost of the test be a factor in keeping you from taking it.

Begin Thinking About and Writing Essays

If you are **really** feeling ambitious, you can begin writing essays for colleges or scholarship applications. A number of colleges and scholarships require essays to accompany them when you submit them for consideration.

Applications will often ask you submit an essay in which you to talk about your interests, your plans, or your personal history. Some ask you to talk about problems that you have overcome, while others ask you to talk about your greatest accomplishments. Scholarships may ask you to talk about how you will use the money that could be awarded to you, or how receiving the scholarship would be a benefit to you.

It is a good practice to save your work that you do for each essay. Many times you can "recycle" what you have written in one essay for use in another essay or for another application. Talk to your counselor about things you should include about yourself on specific essay questions. Not only could their experience with what people have written about in the past help you, but they might remember something about you, or something that you have done that you have forgotten to include. Your school counselor can be a wealth of information!

NOTES

"College is the reward for surviving
high school."

Judd Apatow

October

Do We Need To Say It?   Sign Up To Take The ACT®/SAT®.

Seriously. If you haven't done it yet, do it. And if you want to do it again, sign up again.

Keep Your Eyes Open For Scholarships

If you haven't done so already, start looking for scholarships, both online and by asking your counselor about them. This is really the beginning of "scholarship season," and you want to make sure you find all the scholarships for which you are eligible.

Submit completed applications for **EVERY** scholarship for which you may be eligible. Don't miss out on a single opportunity to get free money. Completing all those scholarship applications can be taxing. There may even come a point where you will get "sick" of filling out scholarship applications. You will think to yourself, "Why am I even doing this?" Or, you might say, "I don't care anymore!" When you start to feel that way, hang in there and keep on filling them out and submitting them. This feeling won't last forever.

It helps to put things in perspective. Consider this: It may take you 20 minutes to fill out a scholarship application, but for that 20 minutes of work, you may get $500 to $1000 in return! There are two cases with which I am personally acquainted wherein two students each worked for about 10 to 15 hours on filling out a national scholarship. Their efforts paid off. They each received upwards of $20,000 in scholarship money, a free tablet device, and an all-expenses paid trip for four days to Washington D.C.. While there, they met various "A-list" celebrities and were treated to a huge banquet in their honor. Not bad for a few hours of work!

Some scholarships may seem stupid to you. You may think to yourself, "Why would anyone care about how I would react during a zombie-apocalypse, let alone give me money for my story?" In response to your question, "Who cares?!?!?!" If an individual, a company or organization, or whoever wants to give you money for your creative writing and your ability to write about a specific scenario, why do you care? Just write the essay, and submit it! Someone is going to get this money, why not you?

You might say, "But I won't get it. There are hundreds or thousands of people who apply, they won't pick me." Remember the two students who received the $20,000 scholarships? The scholarships they received were national scholarships to which hundreds of people applied and less than 30 students were chosen as recipients for the award from the *nation* each year. Each received the scholarship because their application was impeccable, and because their stories and essays connected with the people on the scholarship committee. Don't sell yourself short and miss out on opportunities.

College Fairs

Many high schools offer opportunities for their students to attend college fairs at this time of year. The title of "college fair" is really somewhat incorrect, because the military, as well as some vocational and proprietary schools, attend these events in an effort to recruit students to their respective agencies as well. Whatever your school might call it, plan on participating.

In addition to getting information about the various post-secondary opportunities available to you at the various institutions in attendance, some colleges and universities will waive their customary application fees if you apply during a college fair. If you are really interested in attending a specific school who is represented at the fair, now is the time to fill out the application form. Remember, just because you apply to a school, or even express interest in it, doesn't mean you are committed to attend.

Why Do Schools Charge Application Fees?

Colleges and universities, as well as other schools, started charging application fees a number of years ago in order to "weed out" those students who weren't serious about applying to the school, but who sent in applications anyway. By charging an application fee, schools can see who is really serious about attending. Additionally, the fee also helps pay for the time and effort involved in processing all those applications. Someone has the job to take care of these things, and the money has to come from somewhere!

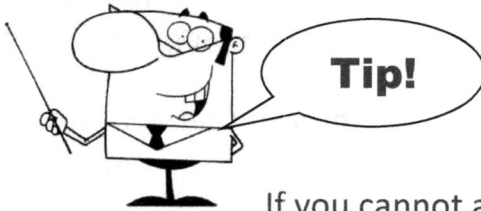

Tip!

If you cannot afford the application fee, talk to your counselor to see if they can get it waived. Sometimes all it takes is a letter from the counselor and schools will waive their application fee.

High School Transcripts

All colleges and universities, some vocational schools, as well as some scholarship applications, want you to submit a copy of your high school transcript with your application. In order to get a copy of your transcript, you will need to pay a visit your school counselor. If the counselor is not the individual in your school who provides you with a copy of your transcript, they will know the proper person in the school for you to contact, as well as the procedure you need to follow for getting a copy. Some high schools have a Registrar who handles all of the transcript requests, so your counselor may direct you to the school Registrar. Either way, the school counselor will know who you should talk to in order to get your transcript sent to the schools of your choice, or to get a copy for you to include with your scholarship applications.

Some schools as well as some scholarship applications require an electronic copy of your transcript to be uploaded to their website. Be aware that you might need to ask your school counselor to help you with this process.

The National Colligate Athletic Association (NCAA®)

If you are considering playing any type of sport in college, you will need to submit a preliminary transcript to the NCAA® around this time of the year. You can submit it later, but it helps to get a transcript submitted early because it allows athletic recruiters to be able to talk to you sooner.

Your school must submit a copy of your transcript on your behalf. It isn't something you can send in yourself. Talk to your school counselor if you are thinking about playing any kind of sport in college so they can get the appropriate information sent in for you.

There is a fee that you have to pay to the NCAA® when you submit your application. You have to pay this fee directly to the NCAA®, and it cannot be submitted by your high school. If you cannot afford the fee, talk to your school counselor and they can request a fee waiver for you. The counselor is required to fill out some information on the NCAA® website in order to facilitate this process. Talk to your counselor and they will be able to help you.

Follow this QR Link to the NCAA® Clearinghouse Registration page. It will take you to the appropriate page.

ISSUE ALERT!

If you are not using the QR code on the previous page, make sure you go to the correct website to register for the NCAA®. Some websites look like they are the correct registration website, but will charge you a fee prior to submitting your information. This is something you can do for yourself without having a third party do it for you.

School Specific Financial Aid Forms

Contact the Financial Aid office at the schools you are considering attending after high school to see if they require you to submit any special financial aid forms at their institution. The FAFSA® (which you have to wait to submit after the first of the year) is required if you plan on receiving any financial aid, but some schools may have their own specific forms that you need to fill out in order to be considered for various scholarships or grants at their school. Check with those schools to see if you will need something special, and talk with your school counselor to see what insights they can provide you.

Finish School Entrance Projects

Depending on the type of school to which you apply, you may have to audition, submit a portfolio of your work, submit writing samples, or send them some other type of project for evaluation. For example, one college's music program requires that students who are being considered for admission into their program submit an original musical composition to review. Additionally, this particular school requires that the piece be between 2-3 minutes long and it has to be accompanied by the written musical score of the composition. If you have a project like this to tackle, you need to pace yourself so that you have plenty of time to get it completed well before the deadline. Procrastination is not your "friend" in this type of situation.

Other schools may request that you audition for their program, particularly music or theater programs. Make sure you check with the school you are interested in attending for these types of entrance requirements to ensure that you are ready to audition when the time comes.

Art schools may require that you submit a portfolio of your work, which is nothing more than a collection of the paintings, drawings, or sculptures that you have created. This is your opportunity to show them you have what it takes to be successful in their programs. Now is the time to pull out all the stops and strut your stuff!

"It is the mark of an educated mind
to be able to entertain a thought
without accepting it."

Aristotle

NOTES

November

With the change of the seasons comes the realization that time is passing, and your school year will soon be coming to an end. Now isn't the time to slow down, however. There are a few things you need to be doing this month to keep you on track, especially before the holidays, so let's start looking at them.

Make Sure You Get Admissions Applications In On Time

Whether it is for scholarships or for admission into college, make sure you keep on top of your applications. Remember to keep a copy of each one you submit, along with the date that you submitted or mailed it.

Post-secondary institutions can receive literally hundreds, thousands, and some, even tens of thousands of applications each year. Therefore, misplacing one application in all of those that come in to an admissions office can be very easily done. An application might be lying on one admissions counselor's desk waiting on a copy of a transcript, which they may already have received, but the transcript for that application could be on another person's desk. It is not uncommon for post-secondary institutions to send you a letter saying that they have not received a component of your application, whether it is your test scores, your transcript, or perhaps your immunization records. When this happens you can get very frustrated because you know you sent the items in to them, but have no way of knowing for sure that they were received or who actually might have received them.

One of the things that you can do to help prevent this confusion is to go to your local "super-store" and purchase blank post cards and print up some confirmation of receipt cards. One side of the card would look something like this:

Name: <u>(Put Your Full Name Here)</u>	
Information Sent:	<u>(List what you have sent them, i.e., transcript, immunization records, etc.)</u>
Date Sent:	<u>(Put the date you sent the information)</u>
Received By:	<u>(Leave this space blank)</u>
Date Received:	<u>Leave this space blank)</u>

The other side of the card would look like this:

Your Name

Address

               Your Name

               Address

Place a stamp on the post card and include it with whatever documents you submit. Repeat this process every time you submit something to an institution. When the information you are sending is received by the school, whoever opens the envelope with your information in it will see the card, and most likely put their name in the "Received By" section, along with the date they received it. Because the card already has a postage stamp on it, the person who receives it will simply pop it into the mail back to you.

The key is to make the process as easy as possible for the person receiving your information to return the card to you. Thus, making sure that the post card already has appropriate postage attached to it, along with it being addressed to you facilitates this process nicely. If you make it overly complicated for them by not including postage or requiring them to address it, you most likely won't get your card returned.

Pace Yourself

Keep checking on when things are due so you can pace yourself in getting items completed and submitted on time. You may find that a number of scholarships are due at exactly the same time. Sometimes students get really frustrated when this happens, and they find themselves staying up late to get the applications finished and submitted before the deadline.

Don't put yourself in this position, because it will definitely cause you undo stress. When you are stressed you become less productive. Pace yourself in getting things done, and do them early so you don't have to worry about them. Remember, procrastination is not your friend.

Register To Take the ACT®/SAT®

If you haven't done this yet, DO IT! You will thank us later!

Follow Up With People About Letters Of Recommendation

Remember those people you asked to write you letters of recommendation/reference? Now is the time to follow up with them. It is likely that some of them have already provided you with a letter, and it is also equally likely that some have not. Some people may have forgotten that you asked them to write a letter for you altogether. Gentle reminders are the best. Remember to thank them for the time that they took (or are taking) in writing you a letter, even if they just write a couple of short paragraphs.

Financial Aid Nights

Most high schools offer some type of financial aid information night or workshops for students and parents to learn more about financial aid and the process used to acquire it. Talk to your counselor about when these informational sessions are available at your school and make plans to attend with your parents or guardians.

Not every school will have a financial aid workshop in November. Some may have them later in the year, or some may have them just prior to the FAFSA® deadline. The advantage to having the workshops after the first of the year is that you can actually file your FAFSA® once you have everything you need, so the information you get from the workshop can be immediately put to use.

Whenever your high school elects to hold a financial aid workshop, you and your parents or guardians need to attend. Such workshops are invaluable to anyone wanting to further their education.

And speaking of financial aid....

Financial Aid: An Overview

For many people, navigating through the world of financial aid is the most mysterious and fearsome aspect of their Senior year. Financial aid.....what is it? How do you get it? What are the secrets!?!?!

The truth be told, it isn't as mysterious as everyone thinks. Let's look at a general overview of the various types of financial aid and then we will talk about the process for getting financial aid. We will also discuss who you need to talk to about issues you may have, regardless of where you want to go to school after you graduate.

Financial Aid: The Four Types

There are four basic types of financial aid; scholarships, grants, work study and student loans. The mistake that people make when defining financial aid is that they only consider scholarships and grants, and don't really consider loans or work study to be financial aid. The federal government, schools, and lending agencies define financial aid as a combination of all four elements, and you need to as well. Let's look at each in a bit more depth.

Grants:

Grants are "free money." This is money that you do not have to pay back. There are different types of grants including the federal Pell Grant for which you can possibly qualify. Many states have grants that they offer to students who are residents of their state as well.

You need to pay attention to the deadlines that your state has in place with respect to specific state grants. The federal deadline for the FAFSA® (more about it in a bit) is currently midnight central time, on June 30th. However, each state has their own individual deadlines for FAFSA® submission as it pertains to state grant eligibility. These deadlines are listed on the federal website https://fafsa.ed.gov. Many of these state level deadlines are well before the June 30th federal deadline, so be aware of what they are for your state.

Scholarships:

Scholarships are also "free money." They consist of money you do not have to pay back…..most of the time.

Each scholarship is unique. Imagine you are a multi-millionaire and you decide that you want to help kids to go on to school after high school. In order to do this, you decide to set up a scholarship fund. You donate a sum of money, let's say 3 million dollars, to a financial management company who takes care of your investment. This company is legally bound to carry out your wishes with respect to how the money is used and dispersed.   The money is invested, and the interest earned on the money is what is used to pay for the scholarships awarded by the fund.

Who decides which students get the money from the scholarship fund? Whomever the person who set up the fund says will do it. It is their money, and they can set whatever parameters on its use that they like. Who gets the scholarships? Anyone who meets whatever criteria set by the person who established the scholarship fund.

So, let's say that with the 3 million dollars you have invested into a scholarship fund, you have decided you want to help people from the school from which you graduated. Now let's say that you really have an affinity for science, so you decide that anyone who applies from your old school has to be going into a science related field in college. Then let's say, you decide that because you have red hair, you only want your money to go to applicants who also have naturally occurring red hair (in other words, someone can't dye their hair in an attempt to get the money.)

Seriously. This can happen. People can set up scholarships with whatever criteria they want as qualifiers. You have to sort through all these details when you apply, but there is no reason you shouldn't apply if you meet all the criteria. (You may be asking how they will know if you have red hair or not? It is not uncommon for scholarship applications to ask that you include a picture. Additionally, the application will probably ask someone to attest to the veracity of what you are saying on your scholarship application....like your school counselor.)

Remember that we previously made reference to the idea that you don't have to pay scholarships back....sometimes. There are occasions where if you accept a scholarship and then you make a decision that is contrary to the specifications of the scholarship, you may have to pay it back as a loan.

Here's an example. Let's say that you accept a scholarship to pay for your schooling to be a teacher, but part of the agreement is that you have to teach in a rural area in Alaska for three years in order to qualify. Initially you agree to teach, but then one year in to your teaching assignment, you decide that you cannot stand the isolation any longer and you resign and move to California.

It can be written into the scholarship agreement that if you don't fulfill your part of the deal, that the money you were given as a scholarship becomes a loan which has to be paid back to the scholarship fund. Make sure that you understand the requirements and conditions of a scholarship before you agree to accept it.

Work Study

One form of financial aid that a number of high school Seniors seem to be unaware of is the federal work study program. This program allows you to earn a specific sum of money at the current rate of minimum wage. Let's say that you fill out your FAFSA® and it comes back that you qualify for $1,500 annually through the federal work study program. As a result, you are eligible to work up to 20 hours per week and get paid the current minimum wage per hour, until you have received the entire $1,500. For example, you may work in an office doing clerical tasks up to 20 hours/week, and you would get paid per hour whatever the current minimum wage is at the time to do that job, until you get paid the $1,500.

There are any number of jobs that you could be hired to do on campus. Perhaps you will work in the residence hall as a residence hall assistant. You could work in the maintenance department, or for food services, and the list continues. The one thing you need to keep in mind is that you can only get a job in an area if an opening exists, just like in the "real world." You may have to take a job that you don't particularly prefer, but doing so may be the only way to get the work study funds for which you are eligible.

What happens when the money is gone? It depends. Some schools will continue to pay you as a part-time student assistant out of a different pot of money. Sometimes, if there isn't any money left in any of their other accounts to pay you, they will have to let you go. You shouldn't look at work study as a sure source of income beyond what you are awarded, so don't depend on it entirely. If you get let go because your money has run out, you may need to get a part-time job off campus to help with your expenses. Actually, it is not uncommon for students to have a work study position as well having another part-time job.

The idea behind the work study program is that you will use the money that you earn through employment to go toward expenses that you incur while going to school. The theory is that, hopefully, you will also save money while you are working to help pay on your student loans. While this is the theory, it doesn't always translate well into reality. More often than not, the money is used for whatever you wish to spend it on at the time. Use your money wisely.

Loans

Loans. The dirty word of financial aid. People don't consider loans as financial aid, but they are. And what's more, loans are often a very large part of a student's financial aid package. If you can make it through college or any other post-secondary educational facility without having to take out a student loan, you will be very lucky indeed.

There are different kinds of loans and the specifics of them change over time depending on the current state of the economy, who is in political office, and a myriad of other factors. For our purposes, we are going to call a loan what it is; money you have to repay to the lender. Having said this, we are going to break the loans down into a couple of different types:

Subsidized Student Loans: Loans which the state or federal government pays the interest on while the student is enrolled in school as at least a half-time student.

Unsubsidized Student Loan: Loans in which the student is charged interest on the loan. While a student does not have to pay on the loan while enrolled in school, interest is being charged and is accruing for later repayment.

Generally, you do not have to start paying back any type of student loan until 6 months after you leave school. The key words here are "leave school." You can leave school for a variety of different reasons and in a number of different ways. You can graduate, take time off, drop out, or even flunk out of school. However when you "leave" school, your time begins ticking, and in 6 months you have to start paying back the loans (unless, of course, you are in the military and are deployed.)

Your Financial Aid Award Package

When you apply for financial aid, the schools put together a package for you consisting of scholarships, grants, work study and loans to help you pay for your education. How do they decide how much of each you are supposed to get? Well, this is where it gets a little more complicated, but not much. In order to get the ball rolling, you need to fill out the FAFSA®.

The Free Application For Federal Financial Aid (FAFSA®)

This is THE form you need to complete in order to get financial aid. J.R.R. Tolkien would probably refer to this as the "One Form to rule them all." If you do not fill out this form, schools will not be able to give you any type of financial aid.

The Free Application for Federal Student Aid, known as the FAFSA®, is somewhat similar in nature to a short version of an income tax form. It has undergone a few changes over the years, but basically it consists of about eight pages of questions that are designed to assess what you and/or your parents can pay, and how much you and/or they will contribute to your education.

When you look at the FAFSA®, you might feel a bit overwhelmed. It can be intimidating, especially if it isn't something with which you are familiar. The key here is to NOT PANIC. It isn't as intimidating as it first appears. You simply have to answer each question truthfully and to the best of your ability, and you will be fine. Keep in mind that there are a number of people around to help you through this process, so you don't have to go through this alone.

The following illustrations are actual pages from the FAFSA®. These are included to give you an idea of what to expect. For the sake of keeping things brief, we haven't included a copy of the entire form.   Remember, it can change from time to time, and we aren't as concerned with giving you specifics as we are giving you a general idea about what to expect.

FAFSA™

FREE APPLICATION *for* FEDERAL STUDENT AID

July 1, 2013 – June 30, 2014

Federal Student Aid | PROUD SPONSOR of the AMERICAN MIND™

Step One (Student): For questions 1-31, leave blank any questions that do not apply to you (the student).   OMB # 1845-0001

Your full name **(exactly as it appears on your Social Security card)** If your name has a suffix, such as Jr. or III, include a space between your last name and suffix.

1. Last name   2. First name   3. Middle initial

Your mailing address
4. Number and street (include apt. number)

5. City (and country if not U.S.)   6. State   7. ZIP code

8. Your Social Security Number   9. Your date of birth   MONTH   DAY   YEAR   10. Your permanent telephone number   (   )

Your driver's license number and driver's license state (if you have one)
11. Driver's license number   12. Driver's license state

13. Your e-mail address. If you provide your e-mail address, we will communicate with you electronically. For example, when your FAFSA has been processed, you will be notified by e-mail. Your e-mail address will also be shared with your state and the colleges listed on your FAFSA to allow them to communicate with you. If you do not have an e-mail address, leave this field blank.

14. Are you a U.S. citizen? Mark only one. **See Notes page 2.**
Yes, I am a U.S. citizen (U.S. national). **Skip to question 16.** ○
No, but I am an eligible noncitizen. **Fill in question 15.** ○
No, I am not a citizen or eligible noncitizen. **Skip to question 16.** ○

15. Alien Registration Number
A

16. What is your marital status as of today? **See Notes page 2.**
I am single ○   I am separated ○
I am married/remarried ○   I am divorced or widowed ○

17. Month and year you were married, remarried, separated, divorced or widowed.   MONTH   YEAR
See Notes page 2.

18. What is your state of legal residence?   STATE

19. Did you become a legal resident of this state before January 1, 2008?   Yes ○   No ○

20. If the answer to question 19 is "No," give month and year you became a legal resident.   MONTH   YEAR

21. Are you male or female?   Male ○   Female ○

22. **If female, skip to question 23.** Most male students must register with Selective Service to receive federal aid. If you are male, age 18-25 and not registered, fill in the circle and we will register you. **See Notes page 2.**   Register me ○

23. Have you been convicted for the possession or sale of illegal drugs for an offense that occurred while you were receiving federal student aid (such as grants, loans or work-study)?
Answer "No" if you have never received federal student aid or if you have never had a drug conviction while receiving federal student aid. If you have a drug conviction for an offense that occurred while you were receiving federal student aid, answer "Yes," but complete and submit this application, and we will mail you a worksheet to help you determine if your conviction affects your eligibility for aid. If you are unsure how to answer this question, call 1-800-433-3243 for help.   No ○   Yes ○

Some states and colleges offer aid based on the level of schooling your parents completed.
24. Highest school your father completed   Middle school/Jr. high ○   High school ○   College or beyond ○   Other/unknown ○
25. Highest school your mother completed   Middle school/Jr. high ○   High school ○   College or beyond ○   Other/unknown ○

26. When you begin college in the 2013-2014 school year, what will be your high school completion status?
High school diploma. **Answer question 27.** ○   Homeschooled. **Skip to question 28.** ○
General Educational Development (GED) certificate. **Skip to question 28.** ○   None of the above. **Skip to question 28.** ○

For Help — www.studentaid.gov/completefafsa   Page 3   Step One CONTINUED on page 4

Step Two CONTINUED from page 4

43. Student's 2012 Additional Financial Information (Enter the combined amounts for you and your spouse.)

a. Education credits (American Opportunity, Hope or Lifetime Learning tax credits) from IRS Form 1040—line 49 or 1040A—line 31. $ ☐☐☐,☐☐☐

b. Child support paid because of divorce or separation or as a result of a legal requirement. Don't include support for children in your household, as reported in question 93. $ ☐☐☐,☐☐☐

c. Taxable earnings from need-based employment programs, such as Federal Work-Study and need-based employment portions of fellowships and assistantships. $ ☐☐☐,☐☐☐

d. Taxable student grant and scholarship aid reported to the IRS in your adjusted gross income. Includes AmeriCorps benefits (awards, living allowances and interest accrual payments), as well as grant and scholarship portions of fellowships and assistantships. $ ☐☐☐,☐☐☐

e. Combat pay or special combat pay. Only enter the amount that was taxable and included in your adjusted gross income. Don't include untaxed combat pay. $ ☐☐☐,☐☐☐

f. Earnings from work under a cooperative education program offered by a college. $ ☐☐☐,☐☐☐

44. Student's 2012 Untaxed Income (Enter the combined amounts for you and your spouse.)

a. Payments to tax-deferred pension and savings plans (paid directly or withheld from earnings), including, but not limited to, amounts reported on the W-2 forms in Boxes 12a through 12d, codes D, E, F, G, H and S. $ ☐☐☐,☐☐☐

b. IRA deductions and payments to self-employed SEP, SIMPLE, Keogh and other qualified plans from IRS Form 1040—line 28 + line 32 or 1040A—line 17. $ ☐☐☐,☐☐☐

c. Child support received for any of your children. Don't include foster care or adoption payments. $ ☐☐☐,☐☐☐

d. Tax exempt interest income from IRS Form 1040—line 8b or 1040A—line 8b. $ ☐☐☐,☐☐☐

e. Untaxed portions of IRA distributions from IRS Form 1040—lines (15a minus 15b) or 1040A—lines (11a minus 11b). Exclude rollovers. If negative, enter a zero here. $ ☐☐☐,☐☐☐

f. Untaxed portions of pensions from IRS Form 1040—lines (16a minus 16b) or 1040A—lines (12a minus 12b). Exclude rollovers. If negative, enter a zero here. $ ☐☐☐,☐☐☐

g. Housing, food and other living allowances paid to members of the military, clergy and others (including cash payments and cash value of benefits). Don't include the value of on-base military housing or the value of a basic military allowance for housing. $ ☐☐☐,☐☐☐

h. Veterans noneducation benefits, such as Disability, Death Pension, or Dependency & Indemnity Compensation (DIC) and/or VA Educational Work-Study allowances. $ ☐☐☐,☐☐☐

i. Other untaxed income not reported in items 44a through 44h, such as workers' compensation, disability, etc. Also include the first-time homebuyer tax credit from IRS Form 1040—line 67. Don't include student aid, earned income credit, additional child tax credit, welfare payments, untaxed Social Security benefits, Supplemental Security Income, Workforce Investment Act educational benefits, on-base military housing or a military housing allowance, combat pay, benefits from flexible spending arrangements (e.g., cafeteria plans), foreign income exclusion or credit for federal tax on special fuels. $ ☐☐☐,☐☐☐

j. Money received, or paid on your behalf (e.g., bills), not reported elsewhere on this form. $ ☐☐☐,☐☐☐

Step Three (Student): Answer the questions in this step to determine if you will need to provide parental information. Once you answer "Yes" to any of the questions in this step, skip Step Four and go to Step Five on page 8.

45. Were you born before January 1, 1990? .... Yes ○ No ○

46. As of today, are you married? (Also answer "Yes" if you are separated but not divorced.) .... Yes ○ No ○

47. At the beginning of the 2013-2014 school year, will you be working on a master's or doctorate program (such as an MA, MBA, MD, JD, PhD, EdD, graduate certificate, etc.)?................................ Yes ○ No ○

48. Are you currently serving on active duty in the U.S. Armed Forces for purposes other than training? See Notes page 2. ... Yes ○ No ○

49. Are you a veteran of the U.S. Armed Forces? See Notes page 2. .... Yes ○ No ○

50. Do you have children who will receive more than half of their support from you between July 1, 2013 and June 30, 2014?... Yes ○ No ○

51. Do you have dependents (other than your children or spouse) who live with you and who receive more than half of their support from you, now and through June 30, 2014? .... Yes ○ No ○

52. At any time since you turned age 13, were both your parents deceased, were you in foster care or were you a dependent or ward of the court? See Notes page 9. .... Yes ○ No ○

53. As determined by a court in your state of legal residence, are you or were you an emancipated minor? See Notes page 9. ... Yes ○ No ○

54. As determined by a court in your state of legal residence, are you or were you in legal guardianship? See Notes page 9. ... Yes ○ No ○

55. At any time on or after July 1, 2012, did your high school or school district homeless liaison determine that you were an unaccompanied youth who was homeless? See Notes page 9. .... Yes ○ No ○

56. At any time on or after July 1, 2012, did the director of an emergency shelter or transitional housing program funded by the U.S. Department of Housing and Urban Development determine that you were an unaccompanied youth who was homeless? See Notes page 9. .... Yes ○ No ○

57. At any time on or after July 1, 2012, did the director of a runaway or homeless youth basic center or transitional living program determine that you were an unaccompanied youth who was homeless or were self-supporting and at risk of being homeless? See Notes page 9. .... Yes ○ No ○

For Help — www.studentaid.gov/completefafsa   Page 5

Keep in mind that you fill out this form online, and that you may not have to answer all the questions that are asked on the paper version. The electronic form has "skip logic," and depending on how you answer one question, you will not have to answer follow up questions related to the first one. For example, if you answer that both your parents are unmarried but are living together, you won't have to answer questions about alternative addresses, etc. This "skip logic" is designed to make the form easier and quicker to complete.

ISSUE ALERT!

Make sure that you do not use ANY website to fill out your FAFSA® other than the official government website, https://fafsa.ed.gov/. If you accidently go to any other website, the site will undoubtedly attempt to charge you to submit your FAFSA®. For the accurate website, you may use the following QR Code.

Once you fill out the FAFSA®, you will receive a report known as the Student Aid Report (SAR). On the

SAR is a number called the Estimated Family Contribution (EFC). The EFC is the amount of money that you and/or your family will be expected to pay regardless of where you go to school. The lower this number is, the more financial aid you may be eligible to receive.

Let's repeat that again. The EFC is the amount of money that you or your family will be expected to pay *regardless of where you go to school*. That means that if you go to Harvard, Yale or Crackatoea Community College, the EFC stays the same. The lower the EFC is, the more financial aid you *may* be eligible to receive, but not necessarily *will* receive.

How does the government use the information on the FAFSA® to calculate your EFC? That's a rather difficult question to answer and is well outside the scope of our discussion. Suffice it to say that there is a formula that is used to make the calculation, and it is a very involved process. The information you provide on your FAFSA®, which includes information from your parents income tax return, how much you and your parents have in savings, how much each of you have in checking, and a number of other things, figure in to the calculation.

The important thing to remember is to answer the questions on the FAFSA® as honestly and accurately as possible. Purposefully altering or withholding information to try and lower your EFC constitutes financial aid fraud, and is punishable by severe penalties and possible imprisonment.

It is important that you and/or your parents try to get your taxes done as quickly after January 1st in order to submit your FAFSA® as soon as possible. If for whatever reason you cannot get your taxes done before the state deadline for FAFSA® submission, don't worry. You can estimate your taxes based on the previous year's income tax return and go ahead and file your FAFSA®. Once you get your income taxes filed, you can provide an update/correction to your FAFSA®.

But What If I Do Something Wrong?!?!?

First of all, stop worrying. It isn't like they are going to send you to jail for making a mistake on this form. You will simply have to submit a correction. As long as you submit the original by the state deadline, you will be fine, and any corrections made later will be taken into account accordingly.

If however you purposely try to scam the government, it is a different story. Federal agents do not look favorably on intentional fraud. They will be able to determine quite easily if you made an honest mistake while filling out the FAFSA®, or if you are intentionally trying to be misleading.

ISSUE ALERT!

If your FAFSA® gets audited don't worry. It doesn't mean that you have done something wrong. A certain percentage of random FAFSA's® are required to be audited each year. If you are selected for an audit you may have to provide a bit more information, but the Federal Government or the school of your choice isn't trying to catch you up in something.

Can I Get An Idea of What My EFC Will Be?

Being the inquisitive creatures that humans are, you are most likely wondering if you can get a "sneak peek" at what your EFC will be. And so, you can. However, you must keep in mind that it will only be an estimate. It is based on preliminary information you provide and should not be considered final. In other words, until you get the *final* official word, you won't know for sure what your EFC truly is.

There are a number of websites that will provide you with this information. Having said that, you should keep in mind that it is always best to go to the source, which in this case is the federal government's web site. Other websites may end up sending you SPAM as a result of using their site.

To find out what your estimate will be, you can go to www.fafsa.ed.gov to find it. Or, you can follow the QR link below and it will take you directly to the website.

Ok....I Know My EFC....So What?

If you went to the website above and entered in your information, you have an estimate of your EFC. Additionally, by using an institution's Net Cost Calculator you have the estimate of the cost of the college. These two numbers will give you an idea of what the cost of attending an institution will be. Here is a simple formula to help you get an approximation of what your financial need will be.

The Cost of The School

Minus (-)   The EFC

= Financial Need

Financial need is where financial aid comes in to play. This is the part that is comprised of grants, scholarships, work study and loans. Let's look at the formula taking these elements into account.

	The Cost of The School
Minus (-)	The EFC
Minus (-)	Grants
Minus (-)	Scholarships
Minus (-)	Work Study
Minus (-)	Loans

Unmet Financial Need

It is entirely possible that you may have an EFC of zero, which is a good thing. It is also possible that you have enough in scholarship money that you do not have to pay anything and will be receiving a "full ride," as they say. What's more, it is also plausible that you could have enough money in scholarships that you actually get paid to go to school, as you end up with more money than the price of the school cost. (If that happens, it can be considered taxable income, and you may need to consult with a tax professional to help you).

Looking at the second formula and using all the listed types of financial aid, you theoretically could end up with a financial need of zero (at least with respect to paying for school.) Aside from grants, scholarships and work study money that you might receive, you will be required to make up the difference between what the school costs and the amount of money you receive.....and this is generally done by taking out more in student loans (or by selling a kidney...but most people prefer taking out a loan ☺).

Special Circumstances

Sometimes in life, things happen. Unpleasant things. People lose jobs, have a parent pass away, parents get divorced or are temporarily abducted by aliens...something. (Please pardon the attempt to make this subject more light hearted.) If you have a special circumstance in your life which has caused you to have a major financial change within the last year, you need to speak directly to the financial aid office at the institution you are planning on attending to make them aware of your circumstances. Any of the aforementioned situations, along with a myriad of others, can affect your financial aid standing, and your EFC. By alerting the financial aid officer at your respective institution, they can help guide you through the process of applying for financial aid while taking your particular circumstances into account.

Another example that is not an uncommon special circumstance is that someone may have no legal guardians and you are living with friends. If such is the case with you, then you need to let the financial aid administrator know this information. They can look at your situation and give you very specific advice, and possibly readjust your financial aid package accordingly.

Other situations which may be considered as special are:

- If one or both of your parents are in jail.

- You have left home because you were being abused.

- You have no idea where your parents are and you cannot contact them.

- You are older than 21 (but less than 24) and are homeless or self-supporting.

All these situations are considered special circumstances and you should discuss them with the financial aid administrator at your selected school.

Keep in mind that you may need to discuss some rather uncomfortable subjects with the financial aid office at your selected school. The thing you need to remember is that financial aid officer is there to help you and, rest assured, they have heard similar stories in the past. Also, everything you tell them is confidential, so don't worry.

Hopefully this brief overview of financial aid and the financial aid process has shown you that it really isn't that complicated after all. The uncertainty of it all is what makes it seem overwhelming at times. The key is to know that you have plenty of people who are available to help you when you have questions. Ask your school counselor, and if they cannot answer your question, they will certainly know who is able to do so.

"Education is the most powerful
weapon which you can use to
change the world."

Nelson Mandela

NOTES

_____

_____

_____

_____

_____

_____

_____

_____

_____

_____

_____

_____

_____

_____

_____

_____

_____

_____

_____

_____

_____

_____

_____

_____

_____

_____

_____

December

In addition to the hustle and bustle that the end of the year brings, the added activities of your Senior year may make this a very hectic time for you. No doubt you are working on or finishing projects for various classes you are taking, attending sporting events, or simply preparing for the holidays with family and friends.

The good news is that the number of things you need to do this month is fairly short. But, just because it is a short list of tasks does not make the items on the list any less important.

Get Your FAFSA ID

You will be submitting your FAFSA® in the next month or so, and in order to do this, you need to obtain a *FAFSA ID*. Setting up a username and password allows you to access your Federal Student Aid records online as well as allows you to electronically apply for financial aid each year.

In order to have things move along as quickly as possible, it is best to get your FAFSA ID early. Basically, this user identification serves as your electronic signature on the online documents associated with your financial aid records. Because of this, you need to keep it secret and you should *never* give your FAFSA ID to *anyone* and make sure to keep it in a safe place. Keep in mind that you are not required to have a FAFSA ID in order to submit your FAFSA®, but it is the fastest way to sign your application and have it processed. Further, having a FAFSA ID is the *only* way to access your federal financial aid data online. You can use the following QR to access the website to sign up for your FAFSA ID.

Talk To Your Parents About Filing Their Taxes

While it is not absolutely necessary for you and your parents to have your taxes completed prior to filling out the FAFSA®, it certainly does expedite things. Talk to your parents about getting their (and your) tax information together and file it as soon as possible after the first of the year.

ISSUE ALERT!

In order for you or your parents to file an income tax return, the company that you or your parents work for has to submit certain information to the federal government. You need to be aware that some companies don't get their information to the Federal Government until the last possible minute, which is January 31st of each year. Unless your parents are self-employed, or do not have to pay income tax, they won't be able to file their taxes until they get the proper information from the company or organization for which they work. So.....if your parents can't file quickly, it isn't their fault. Don't give them grief for something they can't help....

Remember, you cannot file your FAFSA® until *after January 1st of each year*. Filing as quickly as possible and not waiting helps to expedite you getting your Student Aid Report back more quickly. Keep your eye on state deadlines to make sure you get your FAFSA® filed on time.

> **Tip!**
>
> Even if you think you are not going on to school after graduating from high school, you should STILL fill out a FAFSA®. You might change your mind at the last minute and decide to go on to school. If you wait too long, you may miss out on scholarship money that you might have otherwise received.

Keep An Eye On The Mail

Early admission notices begin to come in around this time of year. This means that if you have applied to a school by now, they may have reviewed your information and may have *provisionally* accepted you as a student. Why provisionally? Because you will not be fully accepted by an institution until they receive a final transcript from your high school, and you cannot get a final high school transcript until after you graduate high school. Once you graduate, your school will send them a copy of your final transcript so that you may be fully admitted.

If you are playing sports, you may also receive a document called a "Letter of Intent." A Letter of Intent is a formal commitment by you to attend an institution. There are penalties if you sign a letter of intent to attend an institution and then elect not to attend. Penalties may include losing a percentage of your future eligibility to play in, as well as possibly losing scholarship money. As they say on the National Letter of Intent website, "Know the rules before you sign."

Keep Looking For Scholarships

This month is generally when the first wave of scholarship due dates come, so keep your eyes open for any scholarship deadlines that may be sneaking up on you. Also, keep looking for additional scholarships that may become available. Some scholarship applications are released for availability during this month and you don't want to miss out on any of those. Constant vigilance for any new scholarships that might be available is key.

NOTES

_____

_____

_____

_____

_____

_____

_____

_____

_____

_____

_____

_____

_____

_____

_____

_____

_____

_____

_____

_____

_____

_____

_____

January

January is here and surprisingly things will begin to move very quickly from this point forward. This is the month that you will need to work on your FAFSA® and get it submitted. Now is also the time when you need to seriously start deciding which school you want to attend when you graduate, if you are planning on attending one. So...let's get started.

Gather Your Information For The FAFSA®

You should be aware that completing the FAFSA® is going to require that you provide quite a bit of information. In order to make things easier on yourself, it is good to have this information on hand before you actually begin filling out the form. Be ready to provide your name, date of birth and address, as well as information about the institution or institutions you are considering attending. If you list an institution on the FAFSA® that you end up choosing to not attend, don't worry. Just because you list a school for consideration doesn't obligate you to attend that institution. If you decide to attend an institution that you didn't list initially, simply log back in using your FAFSA ID, and add the new school. The new institution will then be able to pick up your information.

Below is a list of the things you will need in order to complete the FAFSA®.

- Your social security number.

- Your parent's social security numbers if you are a dependent.

- Your driver's license number, if you have one.

- Your alien registration number, if you are not a U.S. citizen

- Federal tax information or tax returns, which includes IRS W-2 Information for you and your spouse (if you are married) and for your parents (if you are a dependent student).

- IRS Forms 1040, 1040-A or 1040-EZ.

- Foreign tax returns (if you have them).

- A tax return for Puerto Rico, Guam, American Samoa, the U.S. Virgin Islands, the Marshall Islands, the Federal States of Micronesia, or Palau (also if you have them).

- The amount of cash you have available.

- Savings and checking account balances.

- Investments, including stocks and bonds and real estate (not including the home in which you live).

- Business and farm assets for you, and for your parents, if you are a dependent student.

- Records of your untaxed income, such as child support received, interest income, and veterans non-education benefits for you and for your parents if you are a dependent student.

It is of the utmost importance that you keep copies of these records. Do not send your only (or last) copy of anything to any school or to the government. Keep a copy of everything.

File Your FAFSA®

Once you have your information gathered, and as soon as possible after the first of January, file your FAFSA® by going to www.fafsa.ed.gov. Remember, do not use any other websites to register for the FAFSA® other than www.fafsa.ed.gov. Other websites may want to charge you to submit your application, saying that they will review it for you, or offer multiple other enticements in order to get you to use them. DON'T DO

117

IT! They will do nothing more for you than a financial aid officer at the institution you are attending will do for you for FREE. Use the web address above or you can use this QR link to access it directly.

If you need assistance completing your FAFSA®, talk to your school counselor. It is important to note that your school counselor is NOT a financial advisor, and as such cannot (and should not) complete your FAFSA® for you. What your counselor CAN do for you is to refer you to someone who can assist your properly, such as a financial aid officer at your institution of choice or perhaps a local tax preparation professional.

Deciding on a School

Deciding on a school is not always an easy process. It is not uncommon for students to come to the point of tears because they cannot decide on which school to attend. Here's a little technique to help you make the decision. Many students have found this technique to be very helpful.

First, make a chart like this one:

School Name

Positives		Negatives	
Attribute	(+) Points	Attribute	(-) Points

Next, begin brainstorming and list all the positive attributes about the school that come to your mind. It is important that you list them all, even if they seem silly to you at first, (or seem silly to anyone else, for that matter). This is your list, and it deals with your perceptions, so don't be concerned about what someone else might think of your reasons. Keep in mind that you don't need to have a complete and thorough list from the very beginning of the exercise. This list can change as you find out new information. You can always add new items or take away things that you have written down previously at any time during this process.

When you list a positive attribute, rate it on a scale from 1 to 10, with 1 being just "OK", and 10 being the "best." After you have finished listing all the positive attributes you can think of, do the same thing for the negative attributes except rate them on how negative the attributes are, with 1 being "not so bad" and 10 being the "worst thing ever."

Assigning a point value on this scale is crucial to the success of the exercise. Don't think about the values of the attributes too much; just go with whatever your gut instinct tells you to put down for them. Again, you can change their values later. The values are all based on **your** personal perspective and **your** opinion.

One thing you need to consider when making your list of attributes is the "X Factor" of the school. An "X Factor" is some appeal that the school has for you to which you that you cannot really assign a name. It could just be the fact that you have wanted to attend this school since you were young. It could be that your parents or grandparents attended this school, and you want to continue the family tradition. The "X Factor" is a mysterious and very personal variable that you need to consider in your deliberation.

After you have completed your list of attributes and decided upon their scores, both positive and negative, add up the columns. When you are finished you should have something that looks like the following. (Keep in mind that your list will look much different than the one provided and you can have as many attributes as you want).

School Name: Randy School of Arts

Positives		Negatives	
Attribute	(+) Points	Attribute	(-) Points
Close to home	+6	No friends going there	-6
Has the program of study I want	+10	Big campus	-4
			-10
Nice campus	+5		
O.K. financial aid package	+3		
X-Factor	+7		
	+31		

School Score : (31 positive) + (10 negative) = 21 Overall Score

Do this exercise for all the schools you are considering attending. When you are finished, you will have a list of schools and their overall school scores. The school with the highest score (from a purely mathematical perspective) is the one that you feel best suits your needs. By adding in the "X Factor" you figure in the appeal that a school has to you, but it keeps things in perspective. Many times students get so caught up in the idea of attending a specific school that they let the appeal of that school overpower the other variables they need to consider, and their decisions become skewed.

As you are doing this exercise, keep in mind that an attribute can be a positive attribute **as well as** a negative attribute simultaneously. For example, let's say that you like a school because it is close to home. You will have easier access to family, friends, and so on. You can also feel that you do not want to attend that school, *because it is close to home*! Family will be to close, and you don't want to be expected to come home every weekend. If you come across a variable that you feel could be a positive and a negative, go ahead and write it in both columns as a positive and a negative. The only thing you have to do is figure out how much of a positive it is, and how much of a negative it is as well. The amounts could be different for the same variable in each column. For example the fact that a school is close to home might be a +6 in the positive column, while simultaneously being a -4 in the negative column.

This technique expands on the old "pros and cons" technique that so many people have heard about, and perhaps you have used. The problem with simply using pros and cons is that you don't take into consideration how much of a positive the pros are to you, or how much of a negative the cons are. Simply creating a list of the positive and negatives isn't much help. By adding weight to each of the variables, you will get a clearer picture and hopefully be able to make a more accurate and decision.

Be aware that although many students have used this technique and have found it helpful, others have tried it, and disagreed with the results they obtained. How can you disagree with results that you come up with yourself based solely on your own opinions?

When this happens it is usually the case that students are so drawn to a particular school that they forget about limiting the effect of the "X-Factor" in their minds. Instead of looking at things objectively, they are influenced by their heart instead of their head. This is quite common in all other walks of life, so it should come as no surprise that this will also be the case in the selection of a school. In spite of the results, and even though we have considered the "X-Factor" in the calculations, students may still feel pulled to a particular school in spite of what their brain is telling them. This exercise is a very data drive method of making a decision, and more often than not, emotions do come into play when putting the results into action.

What happens when students don't listen to the data? Humans are interesting creatures in that they are prone to make up their mind about something and then rationalize about why their choice was the correct one after the fact, and many times in spite of the data. There is also a phenomenon that exists where presenting someone data that is contrary to that individual's point of view only strengthens their belief in their perspective. How does this apply to college selection?

Often times students end up going to the school they wanted to attend and were drawn to from the beginning, even though they cannot justify why they should attend that school. Equally often, those students attend the school for a semester, or perhaps a year, only to find that they don't really like it as well as they thought they would. At this point one of two things happens. Students either transfer to another school, or they quit school entirely. Rarely do they stay somewhere they are miserable.

It is always best to go through the decision making process and not simply rely on your feelings about a school when you are making a decision about where to attend. Be practical. Use the "X Factor" as the emotional draw of the school, but *limit it* on a scale from 1 to 10, and apply that scale to all your school choices. Take in to account what your heart wants, but don't discount the facts when making your decision as well.

NOTES

_____

_____

_____

_____

_____

_____

_____

_____

_____

_____

_____

_____

_____

_____

_____

_____

_____

_____

_____

_____

_____

_____

_____

_____

"The direction in which an education starts a man will determine his future life."

Plato

February

It seems like that it is during this month or the next is when most students finally come to the realization that their Senior year is quickly coming to a close. Now is the time when you need to be aware of emotional tensions that may arise and stay focused.

"Senior-itis" begins to get worse from this point on to the end of the year, so make sure you keep yourself in check. You may begin to hear your friends talk about not wanting to do anything school related, or talk about the fact that they just want "it" to be over. These are all signs that "Senior-itis" is starting to spread among your peers. Be careful! It is very contagious!

Watch For Your Student Aid Report (SAR)

This is the month (or perhaps around the first of next month) that you should begin watching for your SAR if you have not already received it. Remember that the SAR has your Estimated Family Contribution (EFC), which is the amount of money that you and/or your family will be expected to pay for your education wherever you elect to go to school.

Another thing to keep in mind is that the SAR does not include the amount of Financial Aid that you will receive. Financial aid packages are determined by the individual schools to which you applied. So, when you see the EFC and it is more than you expect it to be, don't panic.

The SAR is an important document. When it arrives, make sure you review it and be ready to submit corrections if necessary. Again, keep it easily accessible and in safe place, perhaps storing a copy of it on a flash drive.

Be Aware Of Deadlines and New Scholarship Opportunities

As always, you need to keep an eye on any deadlines that might be occurring during this month. Don't let anything sneak by you.

Also, while local scholarships may be available at any time during the year, many start coming out about now. Watch for these. Check with your counselor to keep updated on any new scholarships that might be available.

Refine Your School Choice

If you really are torn between schools, and aren't sure which one you would like to attend, here's an additional tip in using the decision making technique that we discussed previously. Don't look at your original school attribute lists. Start fresh. Use the same technique, but do it as if you have never done the exercise previously.

After you have repeated the exercise and exhausted all your thoughts about the pros and cons (along with their respective point assignments), look at your original information sheets. Are the point assignments similar? Are they different? Did you think of all the same points? Did you leave some off, or did you think of some new ones that you hadn't added previously?

Doing the exercise more than once can help clarify your thoughts. If you really wanted to get into the mathematical spirit of the exercise, you could average your scores from each school together from the first and second time you did the exercise and see what you get.

The point of these exercises is that it actually makes you think about your choices in depth. Whether or not you actually decide to "go with the data" and choose the school that "wins" mathematically is up to you. At least you have given thought to your schools of choice, and it cannot be said that you haven't.

NOTES

March

It is during this month, more than any other, that students begin to panic. They realize that graduation is coming and that they will soon have to step into the "real world." Students begin to think about the fact that they might need a source of transportation once they graduate, insurance, home goods, even small things like deodorant, toothbrushes, shampoo, and other items for living life on their own after graduation. Irrespective of whether a student is getting a job once they graduate from high school or going on to school, to many this can be a very stressful time.

The most important thing to do when you start getting stressed about the circumstances and conditions of life beyond graduation is to relax. In counseling, when people let their emotions get the best of them and they start into a panicked frenzy of negative "what ifs," we call this "catastrophizing."

When you start to feel overwhelmed and find yourself thinking about all the bad "what-ifs," you need to stop. Instead try to only think about *good* "what-ifs."

Here's an example of the bad "what ifs:" "What if I go to school and flunk out!?! What if I end up owing all of this money, and I don't have anything to show for it!?!" Let's reframe that bad "what if." Instead, look at it this way: What if you go to school, graduate and are successful? What if you get a really good paying job, and you end up paying off your student loans more quickly than you anticipated? What if, when you go to school, you meet the love of your life?

Don't let your life be controlled by the bad "what-ifs." Focus on potential positive outcomes and keep things in perspective. It is true that it can be difficult, but know that all of the things you are feeling are a result of fear of the unknown. It is OK to be afraid. Just don't let the fear control you.

Another thing that people do when they become overwhelmed is that they have a tendency to look at each and every little thing they need to do, and they feel compelled that they should bring all these little tidbits of things they need to accomplish in to order NOW. When you find yourself looking at the big picture and feeling as if you cannot accomplish it all, it helps to begin to break things down into manageable steps. There is an old saying, "How do you eat an elephant?" The answer? "One bite at a time."

Focus on small steps that allow you to get the bigger things done. The concept of One Little Thing (OLT) helps with this. The idea is that you do One Little Thing each day to help you accomplish your goal. For example, my wife and I love to do landscaping around our house. We have several beds of bushes and flowers all around the premises. Every year we try to do one or two small additions to the landscaping; nothing huge or overwhelming, just something small. Over the years, the additions have added up nicely. The point is that we keep at it. The sum of your efforts will pay off in the long run.

For you, if you do One Little Thing every day toward the tasks you need to accomplish before you graduate, you will find them to be far less overwhelming. For example, instead of getting every scholarship application you have to complete filled out in one or two days and stressing about them, give yourself plenty of time to finish them. Perhaps you could only do half of one scholarship application one night, and finish the other half of it the next night. Pace yourself.

I once had a young lady who was so overwhelmed by all the things she needed to do to get ready to move into an apartment after graduation (an apartment which she hadn't found yet) that she was in tears. She was caught up in thinking about all the things she needed to buy like sheets, cups, plates, forks, spoons, pillows....and the list went on and on. She had herself so worked up that she was almost in a panic.

The thing that makes her case so interesting is that, she was *five months* away from graduating. She had herself worked up about things that she had plenty of time to take care of, but she was thinking about getting everything she need to do done NOW. In her mind, if she didn't have everything taken care of immediately, she was going to fail. By considering everything simultaneously, she became overwhelmed.

As a means to help put things in perspective we took time to write down everything she could think of that she needed to do. From there, she was asked to pick out something that she could take care of that day - nothing big, something small. She picked out a few things, and from that smaller list she was asked to pick just one of items to do that day. We then talked about how many days she had to get everything done on her list, and we looked at the fact that if she did one thing every other day, she would still have plenty of time to get everything taken care of by mid-summer, which was well before she needed to have everything finished.

So when you find yourself starting to stress. Stop. Relax. Go talk to your counselor. They will be able to help you put things into perspective. Slow down...breathe......it will be alright.

If You Haven't Done It, Plan A Campus Visit

Even if you have taken a campus tour, perhaps plan another visit. The spring of the year is a wonderful time to visit school campuses. We cannot overemphasize the importance of actually going to a campus before you make the decision to attend a school. The campus visit makes all the difference in the world when it comes to making the right decision.

You may also find another campus visit is helpful right now especially if you are torn between two schools. Actually immersing yourself in the campus for a day can help clarify things for you.

Also, by visiting a campus more than once you can get a feel for it during different times of the year. Having this little bit of information can be a tremendous asset when it comes to making your final decision about where to attend.

Check With Financial Aid Offices

It is always a good idea to call periodically to check on any issues that may arise with your financial aid. While you shouldn't call every week, it is good to check with the financial aid office at the institution you plan on attending to make sure everything is okay, and that they have all the paperwork submitted that you need.

When you call, ask them if or when you need to speak to them next. Ask them what next steps you need to take care of with them. They will tell you if you need to check on something, or if you can relax. Remember, this is their job, so let them worry about the details. Do as they instruct you to do, and you will be fine.

Tip! Be nice to the people in the financial aid office. They deal with every single person who gets financial aid, and work with each of them to make sure they get the most out of their dollars. They take the time to listen to each individual's story and try to help people resolve any questions they might have. A job in a financial aid office can be quite frustrating. A little kindness and patience on your part can go a long way when you talk to these people.

Being kind to the people in the financial aid office may also make a difference in how hard they work to help you. Remember, as Ben Franklin said, "Tart words make no friends; a spoonful of honey will catch more flies than a gallon of vinegar."

Award Letters

At some point during the next few months, you will likely start getting "award letters" containing the amounts the institutions are offering you as a financial aid package. Some of these letters have a deadline, and the award letter you received must be signed and returned to the institution within a certain timeframe if you plan on accepting their financial aid package.

Be mindful of these dates, because an offer may be withdrawn if you don't get the letter signed and back to the school by the deadline. You don't want to lose any funds because of a missed deadline!

Only Take The Loans You Need

One of the biggest mistakes students make when dealing with financial aid is that they take out more in student loans than they actually need. Just because you CAN get thousands of dollars more than you need to pay for school doesn't mean you SHOULD take the money. At some time you WILL have to pay the money back to the lender.

You can limit the amount of money you borrow. If a college offers you $31,000 in loans over the course of your undergraduate career, and you only need to borrow $10,000, simply take what you need. When considering how much you actually need to borrow you will need to make some decisions. For example, do you need a new computer or can make do using the computers available in the school's library? Do you absolutely need new books, or could you be okay with books that are used? Make wise decisions and only accept the amount of loans that you absolutely need.

Having said all of this, you also don't want to make the mistake of taking out too little money in loans. It is better to take out money you will need using student loans than it is to need money and then not have it. Some students then use credit cards to make up the difference, and get themselves into a mess. Using credit cards can be a dangerous thing, and they can saddle you with a level of debt that can take you a lifetime to eliminate.

You may have heard of people filing for bankruptcy when the fall on to hard times financially. Bankruptcy is where you legally declare that you don't have the money or the means to pay your bills. By an order of the court debt can be significantly lowered, and in some cases excused altogether.

If you think that filing for bankruptcy will get you out of paying your student loans, think again. Educational debt is almost impossible to escape. Claiming bankruptcy usually doesn't excuse educational debt, so if you fall into financial disrepair and file bankruptcy, you will still be responsible for any debt that is related to educational loans. Schools are tenacious about getting their money back that you borrowed. They can do a number of things to collect on the debt. You could possibly have your future wages garnished, face debt collection law suits, loose income tax refunds or lose access to your Social Security Benefits. Educational institutions and the federal government are serious about getting their money back, and will go to great lengths to get it back if you borrow it from them.

The point is, simply don't take out loans for more money than you need. Andrew Josuweit, CEO of Student Loan Hero, put it best when he said, "The last thing you want to do is rack up a lot of debt in law school and then all of a sudden you can't pass the bar exam." (The bar exam is the test that law students must pass in order to become a licensed attorney and actually be considered a lawyer.) What he means is that if you borrow a bunch of money to become a lawyer, and then can't pass the test to be one, you are going to have a lot of money to pay back to someone. Therefore, only take out what you can afford to pay back.

After reading all of this, do student loans seem a bit scary? Are you reluctant to take out a student loan now? The point of giving you this information isn't to scare you away from using student loans. Most likely, you are going to need them. If anything, the point of telling you this is to help you to understand the seriousness of the obligation you will enter into with the lending agency. Use a loan wisely, and you will be fine. Don't just, "take the money and run," or think that it is like other types of consumer debt you can escape. It isn't.

Consider this: A hammer can be a dangerous tool. You can smash your fingers with it, resulting in possible surgery to correct the damage inflicted by the injury. Hammers can tear through a wall, smash rocks, and can cause any number of personal injuries. So, should you simply not use a hammer because it is potentially dangerous? No. Use the hammer, but respect what it is capable of doing, and know what the consequences are if you misuse it.

Just like the hammer, loans are powerful tools. Used correctly they can create wonderful things. However if you aren't careful, both loans and hammers are capable of creating a mess of things around you.

Don't be afraid of taking a loan. If you do, do so wisely and with forethought. Loans are not something to be feared, but they certainly need to be respected.

Summer Job?

If you are interested in finding a job over the summer, now would be a good time to start looking for one. Start asking around to see if anyone knows of any summer jobs that you might like. Ask your parents, aunts, uncles, friends, and so on. Use your social media connections to see if anyone knows of anything that might be available. Also, look in local newspapers, flyers on bulletin boards, or simply look for help wanted signs on businesses fronts.

One source of overlooked summer employment is actually at the institution you wish to attend. They may be able to hire you during the summer months, especially if you plan to start school during the summer. Check with them, and see what they say.

Another potential source for summer employment is at national parks, forests, monuments, and amusement parks. If you want to do a bit of travel and sightseeing while earning some money for school, this might be up a viable option worth considering.

NOTES

April

By this time, you should have a fairly good idea of where you want to attend school and what you are going to be doing after you graduate from high school. Now is the time to start putting the final touches to everything you have been working on all year. It is, as they say, "time to get down to the nitty-gritty."

Make Your Decision

If you have not made a decision about where you plan on attending school next year, you have put it off for about as long as you can. It is time to make the decision as to which school you want to attend and let them know. Many times, schools require housing deposits or other such fees to be paid by this time of year. If your school requires such a thing, you need to get your deposit taken care of as soon as possible.

Let Schools Know If You Are Not Attending

In addition to selecting a school and letting them know if you are planning on being one of their newest students, you also need to let the other schools to which you have applied know that you will not be attending.

Admissions departments at colleges and universities are very numbers oriented. They like to have an accurate count of students who plan on coming to their schools in the fall. It is courteous to let them know your plans. Not only is it a matter of courtesy to let them know that you are not planning on attending their school, it also prevents those awkward conversations from occurring when they call you because they think you are still planning on attending their institution. Further, they may be holding money for you for a scholarship which they can now award to someone else because you are not going to be using it. It only takes a moment to call them and tell them you are not planning on attending. If you don't want to call them, you can always send their admissions department a letter, or an email letting them know. Either way, be courteous and let them know you aren't planning on attending their institution.

Find Out Dates For Registration

Sometime around this time of year, many schools will begin having early registration dates for incoming students next year. Check with your admissions representative or on the college website to see what those dates might be, and make appropriate arrangements accordingly if you wish to attend.

Some colleges or universities may bring the registration to you at your high school, particularly if they are in close proximity. These are all things your school counselor will know, so talk to them to find out what options are available.

Testing

Another thing that can happen during your orientation (more about that later) or registration, is that you can be tested if necessary. Depending on your ACT® or SAT® scores, you may be required to take a placement test to determine what classes you need. Different schools use different placement tests, and they can last anywhere from 30 minutes to 3 hours, depending on how many tests you need to take, if you have to take any at all.

Let's say that a school requires a minimum score of 18 in English on the ACT® to be allowed to take their introductory English class, but you only score a 16. Most likely before the school can schedule you for any classes, you will be required to take a placement test to see in what English level class you need to be placed. The good news is, that if you score higher on the placement test than you did on the ACT®, you could "test out" of an entry level English course. Generally schools take the highest score on whatever test you take in order to make these determinations. This holds true for other subject areas as well.

Be aware that at some schools, if you score lower than the minimum required ACT® or SAT® score, and you score lower than the minimum required score on the school's placement test, you may be required to take what is called "developmental" or "subject enhancement" classes. These are classes that are designed to provide you with the training to get you up to the performance level in that subject area that you need to be operating at in order to be successful in the entry level courses. Generally these developmental or subject enhancement classes do not count toward the required amount of hours necessary for graduation from the institution.

Sometimes you will hear students refer to subject enhancement classes as "bone head" classes. This casts them in a negative light, and isn't really a fair label. Not everyone is good in every subject. If you test low in a subject area, the college wants you to be as successful as possible, so they give you these classes to help you succeed. Instead of looking at them negatively, consider what they really are, which is another class to get you one step closer toward your goal of graduation.

Some four year colleges and universities may also require that in order for you to be fully admitted, that you take these lower level courses that you need at a community or junior college. If this is the case, don't fret. Many people do this, and it is just part of the process of getting through school.

Housing

Housing can be a confusing and sometimes frustrating issue for students. The trend is that colleges and universities are wanting students to live on campus for their first few years in school. As such, schools make staying in the residence halls a requirement of admission to their institution, and charge fees accordingly.

It is really no secret that schools try to keep you on campus. The rationale schools provide you for wanting you to live on campus for at least a few years is that living on campus facilitates you becoming more involved in campus life. Research shows that students who are more involved in campus life are more likely to stay in school, and thus graduate. This is not only helpful to you, because you get a diploma, but it is also helpful to the schools because they have higher retention and graduation rates, which are both used for funding purposes and as recruitment tools. Thus, schools facilitate your involvement by mandating that you live on campus. Some schools will only allow you to live off campus if you actually live with your parents, and then only within a certain distance from the school. You will most likely have to fill out a form requesting that the school waive their residence requirement if you plan on living with your parents, even if you are a "local."

At this time of year, schools may require you to make a housing deposit if you plan on attending their school and living on campus. Check with your admissions representative to see how you go about doing this.

"Education is our passport to the future, for tomorrow belongs to those who prepare today."

Malcom X

NOTES

_____

_____

_____

_____

_____

_____

_____

_____

_____

_____

_____

_____

_____

_____

_____

_____

_____

_____

_____

_____

_____

_____

_____

_____

_____

"There is no substitute for hard work."

Thomas Edison

May - The Summer

You made it! Sometime during May or at least in the month of June, you will graduate from high school. It has been a long process, but you have arrived. Take some time to let it soak in that you are no longer in high school. You have arrived.

Now that you are about to graduate, or have graduated, you need to do a few things to make sure that you have no hiccups in your plans. Let's examine some of these items.

Notify Your High School Counselor Where You Plan To Attend

If you haven't already, tell your high school counselor where you plan on attending school when you graduate. They need to know where to send your final high school transcript. If the school you have selected does not receive your final high school transcript, they cannot officially fully admit you.

Also, if you are planning on participating in a sport in college, you need to make sure that your counselor sends a copy of your final high school transcript to the

NCAA®. You won't be eligible to play, or perhaps even take part in practices, if your transcript isn't received in a timely manner.

Make sure that you get everything taken care of before the counselor leaves for the summer. Once the counselor leaves for break, it may be some time before they return to their office to process requests. Letting them know what you need them to do before your last day of school is the best plan.

Check On Financial Aid Paperwork

Unless you have gotten the final word on your financial aid paperwork from the financial aid office, you should check with them to see if they need you to file any additional paperwork such as an income verification form, dependency status verification, or anything else. Sometimes they may need a letter from your school counselor if you have a special circumstance.

Again, if your financial aid office asks you to submit additional paperwork, it isn't because they suspect you are trying to scam them or that you have done something wrong. They are mandated by the Federal Government to spot check and "audit" a certain percentage of all their students entering each year.

What Do I Need To Do If I Have A Disability And Want To Go To School?

If you have a documented disability and have a 504 Plan, an Individualized Education Plan (IEP) or whatever your school district refers to them as, you need to add a few additional steps with respect to what you need to do in preparation for entering school next year.

It is recommended that during a campus visit or at the very least during your orientation process that you take a copy of your 504, IEP (or whatever your district calls it) with you. You need to let someone at the school involved in the admissions process know that you need to speak to the individual on campus who is in charge of taking care of students with disabilities. Generally there is someone designated on campus to handle accommodations for students with disabilities, both in terms of educational and physical accommodations.

One thing you need to be aware of is that accommodations on a college level are not the same as the accommodations you have received in high school. The same set of rules don't necessarily apply, and the accommodations you are eligible to receive in college can be vastly different from what you have received up to this point. Yes, colleges and universities do have to offer accommodations, but what is defined as a "reasonable accommodation" in college is generally not the same as it is in high school. You will find that some accommodations may be the same, such as extended time for exams or isolated test administration if you have a learning disability, but you won't get the degree of assistance that you did in high school. You may not get tests read to you, you may not have someone provide notes for you, you may not have professors who provide alternative assignments, and so on. Be prepared to discuss changes in how accommodations are made at the institution you plan on attending.

Learn Some Life Skills

Now is the perfect time for you to learn a few simple life skills for living on your own. For example, if you haven't learned how to do your own laundry, now is the perfect time to do that. Whether you get a job or go to school, you need to be able to do your own laundry. Have someone teach you this very simple task. You are a grown up now, so now you should learn about the things you need to do in order to function on a day to day basis.

Lean how to iron your clothes. You may not need to iron your clothes to go to class, but perhaps you will want to go out on a date, or dress up for a school function at some time. Knowing how to iron your clothes will have you looking neat and impressive.

Another thing you should consider learning is how to balance a checking account. Simple financial skills, like keeping track of how much money you have, will be something you need to know before heading off into the "real world." Many times students don't realize how these things work because their parents have always taken care of their finances for them.

Also, learn to cook some simple meals. You don't have to be a gourmet chef, but it will comfort your parents to know that you won't go hungry, and that you have more options for feeding yourself than just eating Ramen Noodles or living off of fast food.

If you have a vehicle, you need to learn about routine maintenance tasks you need to be doing in order to assure that it stays in running condition. Know when you need to have the oil changed, or the tires rotated. Keep track of inspection dates as well as when your tags expire. Knowing simple little things like these will go a long way toward eliminating major headaches down the road.

What are some other things you could learn to make your life easier? Talk to your parents or your counselor about suggestions they may have for you.

Orientation

Orientation is when your new school brings you onto campus to give you an idea of how things work. You may get an extended campus tour, receive further information on financial aid, learn about the campus health center, perhaps get your college ID, possibly get a copy of your schedule, and so on. Orientations are the time that it is easiest for you to get quite a bit of the details taken care of for you to attend your new school.

An orientation can last a few days, or perhaps over the weekend. It all depends on the school. Many times you get to know other students through various activities, meet your advisor, break up into groups and go through various informational items you need to know as you start your college experience. Some schools have orientation immediately prior to the beginning of the school semester, and when you finish orientation you start classes the next day. Others may give you a brief break to return home prior to starting back to school and beginning classes.

How your orientation plays out all depends on the philosophy that your new school has with respect to keeping students involved and on campus. Some schools adhere to the idea that they don't want students to return home after orientation for fear that the student will elect to not come back to school! Other schools feel that it is in the best interest of the student to give them a small break after an intense orientation to recharge their batteries before returning to classes.

Though some orientations can seem to be a waste of time, they are important. You may get bored during some of the presentations, but you need to stay alert enough to know what is important for you to know, and what doesn't really apply to you.

Admittedly, not all the information at orientation will be relevant to you. Having said that, someone on campus (usually a vice-president, or director of a department) feels that the elements that have been included for discussion are important for you to know. The key is be patient and weed out the good information. The only way you can do this is to stay alert and see what the people have to say.

Some schools do a post-orientation evaluation to see what students enjoyed about orientation and what they didn't. If your school does this, be honest with them on the evaluation. Let them know what you felt was good information, and what you felt to be a waste of time. Only through getting feedback will the schools be able to improve the experience for future students.

Some schools end orientation with a ceremony called a "convocation." A convocation is your official induction ceremony into that school. The idea behind a convocation is that you have a formal ceremony at the beginning of your college career, and then you will have a formal ceremony at the end, i.e., graduation. Not all schools have this ceremony, but if yours does, now you know why.

One thing you need to be aware of is that while orientations can be fun, they can also be overwhelming and stressful. Some students have said they feel like cattle being herded from one place to another during orientation. Others describe their orientation as being swept up in a giant tidal wave.

Many people feel exactly the same about their orientation. You may not realize it by watching them, but the people that are going through orientation with you all have some sense of anxiety. Perhaps they hide it well, but deep down, they are as unsure of themselves as you are.

While orientations can be stressful, you will survive and your life will calm down considerably once the process is over. The good news is others have made it through, and so will you.

Take advantage of this time to get all the information you can, and don't be afraid to ask questions if you don't understand something. Use the opportunity to meet new people, try new things, and (most importantly) have fun!

"The only person who is educated is the one who has learned how to learn and change."

Carl Rogers

Things I Need To Do As I Start The Next Part Of My Life

"Education is the key to unlock the
golden door of freedom"

George Washington Carver

Growing old is a biological
imperative. Growing up is optional.

Daniel A. Reed

The Next Chapter In Your Life

People's lives are about the stories they have and about what they share. It is at this point that I would like to take a brief moment to share my personal story with you.

Whatever you plan on doing after you graduate, one element remains constant, and that is the element of change. The number of people who know exactly what they want to do from the time they are in elementary school through high school is impossibly small. As a counselor who has worked with various groups of people across a number of years, I have only known one person who kept the same plan about what he wanted to do after he graduated from high school from the time he was in grade school. Whenever he was asked what he wanted to do, he would always say, "I'm going to be a radiologist." Guess what? He graduated from high school, and went on to do that very thing.

Everyone else that I have known over the course of the years, myself included, changed their plans a number of times. I changed my major in college six times before I finally settled on what I wanted to do. At first, I was a general studies student, who changed to be a business major, and then I changed to a chemistry major. From there, I elected to become biology major and then I moved on to become a criminal justice major. Finally, I ended up in the behavioral sciences, and found the subject matter so compelling that I graduated with a degree in that area.

Even after I graduated and got a job I still didn't know what I wanted to do. In spite of the fact that I was a professional in the mental health field, I felt like there was something else out there for me that I would find more fulfilling. It was then that I planned on furthering my education and becoming a college professor. And so, I did. And while I really enjoyed teaching and being in the academic world, I still felt like something was missing. So, I elected to become a therapist, sitting in an office and discussing people's issues and problems with them. While I enjoyed it, I still didn't feel like I was fulfilled in terms of my career and personal satisfaction.

Finally, after a number of years, I found the job that changed me and filled the void that I couldn't pinpoint previously. Early in my career, I would have regarded anyone who told me that I would enjoy being a school counselor with much skepticism. Amazingly, I returned to the very same high school from which I graduated to become the school counselor.

When I graduated high school, I had no idea where I was going, or what I would be doing. I had a loose plan, but nothing cast in stone. I certainly didn't believe that I would find myself working in the same school I graduated from so many years prior. If I could talk to myself in the past, I'm quite certain that my younger self would be quite shocked to learn where I finally "landed," in terms of a career. Looking at my high school year book, I was quoted as having aspirations to be a business manager. How things change.

Why am I telling you all of this? Because I want to let you know that it is okay to change your mind, and it is okay to explore your options. It is also okay to make mistakes along the way. All these things add up to something called "life." Keep in mind you may not be able to rely on your parents to pay for your "life experiments," and at some point they might tell you that you are on your own. But, for now, it is okay to question yourself and become more than you are.

Also, don't be surprised if you end up finding your true calling in an area in which you least expect it. I certainly didn't have any desire to be a school counselor, let alone at the very high school from which I graduated. Nevertheless, it has been one of the most fulfilling jobs that I have ever had, and at this point, I wouldn't trade it for anything else.

Consider your options, and don't discount anything as a possibility. You may be surprised at what you can do and what you are capable of accomplishing in order to make your dreams a reality. What's more, you may be very surprised at where you finally "land." Just remember life is a journey and not a destination. Enjoy the ride.

"Learn from yesterday, live for today, hope for tomorrow."

Albert Einstein

Things For Parents To Consider

(in other words, let your parents read this part!)

This can be a difficult time for parents. A student's Senior year can be looked at as a closing of a chapter in that student's life, and it can be disheartening at times. In reality, instead of being a closing of a chapter, it is a launching pad for their future. Take heart, parents. You have done your job, and your child has grown. You will always be their parents, and they will forever be your child.

A child never comes with an instruction booklet when they are born. As the parent, you do the best that you can. While every case is certainly unique, there are a number of things that you can do as a parent to help your child no matter what they plan on doing in the years following high school. Let's examine a few of them.

Help Them With Applications

It is a good idea to help them complete applications and keep up on deadlines associated with those applications. Help them keep track of what they need to get done. The key word here is to **help** them do the applications, not **do** the applications for them. Having students fill out applications on their own is a simple life lesson and allows them to begin learning how to take care of these matters on their own. Check over the applications, help answer questions to which they may not know the answer, but let your child do it. You need to start allowing yourself to let go and let them take care of their own matters, and this is a good place to start.

If you have read through this book to this point, you will notice that the advice and the tips offered herein are **for the student** to do. Nowhere does it say, "Have your parents make a folder for you," or, "Have your parents call the financial aid office." Really the only place it specifically talks about parental involvement is during the act of filling out the FAFSA.

As a parent, you may not like what we are about to say, and we mean no offense. We're just trying to help you realize that your role with your child is changing, and their graduation from high school and entry into the "real world" marks a time for you to consider making changes as well.

Your job as a parent is to prepare your child to take care of themselves, on their own. You will not always be around to take care of things for them, so helping them to learn to take care of issues on their own is an important part of what you are teaching them. This is a time of transition where you need to start letting go, and trusting that you have done all you can to guide them in the right direction. They will need to begin making decisions on their own. They will need to start calling people and taking care of tasks and problems by themselves. We're not saying don't support or help them. What we are saying is simply don't do everything for them. Allow them to learn how to handle issues by taking care of matters on their own. Allow then the opportunity to succeed, as well as to make mistakes. It is through all of this that they will learn.

Look at it this way. If you allow them to start taking care of issues on their own now, you are still there to oversee their progress and to make sure they are handling matters properly. You are still there as a safety net for them in case things become overwhelming. Give them this opportunity to grow and discover things on their own, even if it would be easier for you to do it for them. If you see them going astray in the process, guide them, but let them be the ones "at the helm" by talking with school officials and filling out forms. Giving them the foundation for success is one of the greatest gifts a parent can give.

Attend Financial Aid Presentations With Them

This is the one area with which your child will really need your assistance. Their financial aid paperwork is going to largely be based on your tax returns. (If you are legally not required to file taxes, then they will still need information from you about this as well). Because students have most likely never been exposed to tax returns they can find terms like "W-2's," or, "1040-ez" to be vague or menacing. They won't know what to do, and may have several questions about tax related items. Help guide them through these unknown territories.

Attending financial aid workshops with your child will be helpful for both of you. Most financial aid workshops are set up in the evenings or on weekends, and there are often other sessions aside from the ones at the school, such as at libraries, community centers, or other places. Find out when these workshops are by contacting your child's school counselor. You will be glad you did, and your child will be as well.

Register For A FAFSA ID

In November or December it would be good for you to register for your Personal Identification Number so you can electronically "sign" the financial aid forms and assist with your child's financial aid documents. Follow the QR link below for easy access to the FAFSA application website.

Talk With Your Child About Their Options After High School

If you have never had a serious talk with your child about their options following high school, now is the time to do so.   Even if you never went to college, you can still talk to them about their college plans. There are a number of parents who are simply intimidated by their child's plans for life after high school. Don't be afraid of having this conversation with them. It will help them to know you are interested.

If your child doesn't want to go to school, talk with them about that as well. They may have no idea what they want to do. Talking with you may help them figure out a plan, or at the very least give them an idea about potential options they may want to pursue.

One thing that can be difficult for parents to do is to listen to their children in a non-judgmental fashion when they are talking about their choices. Don't criticize their choices, and just listen. One of the biggest issues children have with their parents is that the child feels that their parent will be critical of them if they are open about their feelings. Keep this in your mind as you open up the lines of communication with your child about their choices following high school.

Don't Be A Helicopter Parent

What is a "helicopter parent?" A helicopter parent is a parent who pays extremely close attention to their child's educational activities once they graduate from high school. They are called "helicopter parents" because they tend to "hover" around their child, or even in some cases the educational facility, to the point of impeding the child's ability to mature, both socially and emotionally, as well as in terms of personal responsibility.

Parents don't always realize they are being helicopter parents. Instead, they feel that they are continuing to take care of their child, which is what they have done for the past 18 years. When you are on the outside and are watching a helicopter parent in action, you become painfully aware that the parent is actually doing their child a disservice, when it is not their intention at all.

The thing that parents must keep in mind is that their child is no longer a child. This is the time in their child's life that the parent must learn to start letting go. You cannot protect them forever. You cannot fix their problems indefinitely. This is the point in your child's life when you have to start letting them make mistakes and take responsibility for the results of their decisions. You need to face the fact that you won't always be around to take care of issues for your child. You need to understand that there comes a point when your child needs to learn to deal with matters on their own, independently of you. How else is the child supposed to learn if you do not let them?

Reflect for a moment back on your own life. How did you learn to take care of issues? By experience. Trial and error. Mistakes and successes. At some point, you learned to problem solve and take care of yourself.

Don't misunderstand the intention of pointing this out to parents. This isn't to say that you shouldn't support your child, or go with your child to important events such as on campus tours, or to registration. You need to show your child support, but you also need to let them begin to flex their muscles of independence. You will be there to guide them, but there is no need for you to maintain control and oversight of them at all times.

Being a helicopter parent actually hinders your child, which is the opposite of what your intention is as a parent. As an example, if your child is going to a job interview, don't go with them into the interview. Let them go by themselves. If you want your child to have any chance at all of getting the job, and you elect to go with them, stay in the car. Don't show your face in the building. Rest assured, the person who gets the job isn't going to have their parents waiting with them for the interview in the reception area. Also, as a parent, what type of a message does it send about your child to a potential employer if they cannot handle an interview on their own?

Another instance of being a helicopter parent is attempting to go with your child into anything related to the military, other than some initial visits with a recruiter. The military will not allow you to go to basic training with your child, nor will they allow you to stay in the barracks with your child while they are taking part in training. Parents have tried this, and are often in for a rude awakening when they are faced with the realities of the world that is outside their control.

Seriously, these things happen. The number of reports of parents who won't let their children go on job interviews or to school without them is growing. Face it folks, you have got to let go sometime. Love them, care for them, but let them grow up and become self-sufficient adults.

With respect to enrolling in a school after high school, here are some tips for the parent:

1. Go with your child on tours of college campuses. Ask questions. Show your child you are interested in their choices.

2. Go with your child to register for classes, but let the advisor do their job and give your child the schedule that works. You are doing your child no favors by telling the advisor that your son or daughter, "doesn't like to get up early, so don't give them an 8:00 a.m. class." The question becomes what would happen if your son or daughter didn't show up to work at 8:00 a.m. when they were supposed to do so? They would be fired. Let this experience help train them for the future.

3. Don't fill out forms, such as the FAFSA® or college applications for your child. Help them fill out the forms, but don't do it for them. Assist them with the task, but have them be the one actually completing the forms.

4. Have your child fill out and submit a Family Educational Rights and Privacy Act (FERPA) release form with the institution they are attending.   This form allows you to discuss anything about your child with the school. If you don't fill out one of these forms, the school will NOT talk to you and CANNOT talk to you in accordance with federal law. Be forewarned, you will not be happy if you call in to speak to someone and they tell you, "I can't talk to you unless your son or daughter gives me permission."

5. Try not to use the rights granted to you by the FERPA release. Just because you CAN talk to your child's school does not mean you should. Remember, being a helicopter parent isn't a good thing.

Without trying to be morbid or make you confront your own mortality sooner than necessary, consider what would happen to your child if you died tomorrow. Who would take care of your child's problems then? Don't you think it is better to prepare them to take care of themselves and be able to make their decisions independent of your influence, rather than leave them with the inability to handle life's more tedious or challenging tasks on their own?

It bears repeating that we are not telling you to refrain from helping your child. The thing that we want you to focus on is helping your son or daughter to become functional adults within society. They cannot do this if you as the parent do not give them the opportunity to grow, even if they don't always want to.

Parents and Their Money

Your child is ready to go to school, and you are paying a great deal of money to make this happen. Let us say that some issue arises for your child at school and you feel compelled to call in and take care of the matter for them. To your surprise, you find out that your child has neglected to put a FERPA release on file with the school, or perhaps they have revoked the FERPA release that was on file. If for whatever reason there is no release on file, you will not be able to talk anyone about anything related to your child at the school.

Being upset about the fact that the school won't talk to you, you righteously inform the school that YOU are the one paying for the child's schooling, and that the school WILL talk to you. You demand that they give you answers!

Be prepared, because they will not talk to you. Not without the release. You see, here's what happens: The law views your payment of the tuition to the school as a gift that you have given your child. Once you have given this gift to them, the money that you used to pay for tuition and fees no longer belongs to you, it belongs to your child. In spite of the fact that the money never went through your child's hands, it still belongs to them. Therefore, it is no longer your money, and you have no say in anything that is attached to it.

Consider this: If you buy a car and put it in your child's name, the car is theirs. The title has their name on it, and not yours. If you call the Department of Motor Vehicles, and ask for information about the car, they will not give it to you. It isn't your vehicle. The same scenario is involved in paying for your child's education. Their name is on the "title," so to speak. They, and they alone, have sole rights to their information, not you.

Parents don't like to hear this, and they usually get very upset when this is explained to them. But even if it does upset you, your feelings are irrelevant with respect to the law. Federal regulations state clearly that your child is an adult, and as such they are entitled to privacy of their financial and academic records.

Think about this: Would you want your cousin to be able to call your bank and ask how much money you have in savings? No! The thought is preposterous. Just because they are a relative of yours doesn't mean they should have access to your information. The same standard holds true for ALL relatives. Once your child graduates from high school and enters a post-secondary educational facility, they are viewed by the law in such a way that their privacy is protected, even from you.

"But I claim them on my taxes," you say! Whether or not you claim them on your taxes is irrelevant. Just because they are a dependent with respect to tax purposes doesn't mean that you have access to all their personal information without a proper release. You may be able to discuss some matters if you claim them on your taxes, but how does the person you have called at the school know your relationship with the student? How do they know you aren't some con artist just trying to get information? When you think about it in these terms, people should be grateful that schools will not talk to anyone who calls, or people who are not properly authorized to have access to information.

Just remember, when you sign the check, it is no longer your money. You have basically given it to your son or daughter, who is in turn using it to pay tuition. The money is gone.

In conclusion, parents...be part of your children's lives, but let them grow up to be independent and be able to take care of themselves. You won't always be around to help them, so prepare them to take care of themselves.

It's Time To Say, "So Long….."

One of the hardest things a parent has to do is to leave their child alone at a school. There have been instances wherein a parent has actually asked to stay the night at the institution of the first few days of their child's college orientation. In some cases, parents have actually had to be asked to leave, go home, and trust that the people at the institution will look after their child appropriately.

The hardest part of letting go is….well….letting go. But once you do it, it isn't as if you won't see your child again. Let them experience life. Let them grow. Let them be independent. Let them make mistakes. Let them learn. Let…go.

Sometimes a parent feels like they should hold on because the child doesn't want to let go of them, emotionally speaking. In such cases, the parent has become the child's security blanket. This isn't healthy for the child, and the parent needs to realize that the clingy nature of the parent/child relationship is doing more harm than good.

Be afraid. But, feel the fear and go ahead and let them go anyway. Remember, you are preparing them for life, and life isn't always about safe situations and well made decisions. Is your child going to disappoint you? Perhaps. Are they going to make decisions of which you don't approve? Absolutely. Will you always be there to clean up their mess? No, you will not. Help them to learn how to cope with things on their own.

You are not going to disappear tomorrow (most likely), nor are they. You will see them again, and they will tell you about all the great things they got to do, the people they have met and all the wonderful experiences they are having. Smile. You are watching your child follow the natural order of things and develop into a wonderfully independent person. You are seeing your child transform into an adult before your very eyes. You have done your job well. Trust in yourself, and trust in them.

I Want My Child To Go To School But They Don't Want To Go!

You think your son or daughter should go on to school, but they don't want to go. Now what? You could MAKE them go, but how successful do you think that endeavor will likely be? You are basically making them go into an environment where you have no control over them or their actions. If you make them do this, maybe they go to class, but maybe they don't. Would you really know? They tell you they are studying, but are they really? Finally, when you are able to coerce a grade report out of your child (Remember FERPA? Schools don't send grades to the parents), you find out that they haven't been doing very well at all. Perhaps instead of seeing a grade report, you get a telephone call one evening telling you that your child has been arrested for something related to drugs or underage consumption of alcohol.

Should you push your children to achieve? Yes. A gentle push is one thing, while a forceful shove is another. As a parent, you may rationalize in your mind that you are pushing your child to go to school, because you have always had to be there to push them to get them to do anything at all. Perhaps you have had to "be on them" to stay on task, or take out the trash, or do whatever it is that you feel that you have had to push them to do.

When it comes to getting an education however, things change. Would you push your child to learn to play the piano if the child had no interest and did not want to learn? Most people would say, "No." "But this is different," you say! "This is their future, and I want them to be successful!"

There are two problems with the last sentence, even though on the surface it seems to be a perfectly well founded statement. Both problems are centered around the fact that your response is about you, and not your child. First of all, the sentence really reflects your own personal standards and not the standards of your child. "You" want them to be successful, but "you" are defining the parameters of their success. Because they are not interested in what "you" think is going to make them successful, perhaps in your mind they have failed, or more importantly, you might feel that "you" have failed.

The second issue is that another person's success is defined by that person, not by you. It makes no difference that the other person is your own flesh and blood. When you start trying to compare yourself or your children to someone else as a measure of success, you, and they, are always doomed to some degree of failure. There will always be someone who makes more money, someone who has a nicer house, someone who drives a nicer car. Success is defined by how happy you are with the life you live. If the choices your child makes about their career and education makes them happy, then they are a success.

Recently at a conference a presenter relayed a story about her son. She said that she insisted that her child was going to go to college in spite of her son's protestation to the contrary. He told her he didn't want to go to college, but instead he wanted to focus on getting certified as a welder. The mother was insistent that the son go to college, and so he did.

She said she thought all was well until she saw his first mid-term report. He was doing terribly. The presenter reported that she had a very serious talk with her son, wherein she "laid down the law to him." Her son assured her that he would start doing better, but brought up the fact again that he didn't think college was right for him. She said that she told him, "You need a college education to be successful."

So, time moved on and the presenter said that later that semester she got a phone call from the school, and her son had been arrested on an alcohol related incident. She stated that she was livid, and that she "preached" at him the entire ride home from the jail about how he was ruining his life and his future. She said she tried to impress upon him the importance of his actions and how they would impact every aspect of his life.

Finally, at the end of a very unsuccessful first year in school, the presenter stated she gave up on her dreams of her son graduating from college and being a success.

She said that she was beating herself up because she felt she had failed him as a parent.

The mother stated that she decided that she was going to have to be very blunt with her child, as if she had not up to this point in time. She told him that if he wasn't going to go to school, he would have to get a job. She said that her son looked at her and said, "Mom, can I go to school to learn what *I* want to learn now?" At that moment the mother realized what she had done. In that "ah-ha" moment, she recognized the fact that she had forced her ideas of what *she* defined as an education on to her son, and subsequently what *she* defined as being successful upon him as well.

The presenter went on to say that her son enrolled at a technical school near their home and that he went through the welding program offered by the school and completed it quite successfully. He was interested in the subject matter and was excited about learning. She said he went on to acquire several welding certifications. The presenter said her son seemed to, "suddenly grow up, right in front of my eyes."

After he completed his schooling, the presenter said that her son went on to work for a pipeline company and to make a very good living. In fact, he now makes more money annually than his parents.

The point of the mother's story was to help the audience realize that trying to force your perspective on your children when they become adults will most likely result in grief and heartache for all parties involved. The mother went on to say that this was a, "very expensive lesson" for her, because she ended up paying for her son's first year in college. She said, "I made a mistake by not letting my son dream his own dream."

The point of all this is a simple one. Don't ignore your children's interests and dreams about their future. Guide them, advise them, but let them make their own decisions. You, as the parent, do not have to bankroll every farfetched whim your child wants to explore. Use your experience to help guide them, and if it becomes a financial burden on you, let your child know that you support them in spirit but that they will have to figure out how to support their dreams on their own. If your child really wants it, they will find a way to make it happen.

Epilogue

So, there you have it. The end. But....it isn't really the end. And it isn't the beginning. The beginning of this next chapter in your life started long before graduation. You and your parents have been preparing for this moment for a very long time.

Hopefully, you are able to use the information in this book and it will benefit you in some way. I wish you all the success in the world. If you have a success story you would like to share, I would love to hear from you. Also, if you feel that there is something that could be included in future editions of this book that would be helpful for students, feel free to share that as well. If you notice any grammatical, punctuation, or syntax errors, let me know! I will gladly give you a shout-out of appreciation on the blog thanking you for your help.

And speaking of blogs, please read *Senior-itis,* my blog, and feel free to leave comments, ask questions, and stay in touch. Your feedback is invaluable to me.

One last thing before I go. I would appreciate it if you would be so kind as to write a nice review for this book on Amazon.com. Doing so would help me out tremendously. Also, please consider purchasing a copy of my other book: *Living in the NOW: A Guide to Living A More Fulfilled Life,* also available on Amazon.com. Your support is greatly appreciated.

Live in this moment. Enjoy the now.

Daniel A. Reed

The important thing is not to stop questioning. Curiosity has its own reason for existing.

Albert Einstein

"We all change. When you think about it, we're all different people; all through our lives, and that's okay, that's good. You've gotta keep moving, so long as you remember all the people that you used to be."

The Doctor
Doctor Who Episode 241
"The Time of the Doctor"

Glossary

Academic year - The school year that begins with autumn classes. The academic year for most colleges and universities in the United States starts in August or September.

Acceptance - The decision for an institution to enter into a condition wherein the individual who has applied to an institution is now considered to be a student of that institution.

ACT® - These letters are acronyms for the American College Test This assessment is designed to measure a student's level of knowledge in basic areas such as math, science, English and social studies. Colleges may require the results of either the ACT® or SAT® before granting admission.

Admission - Admission is the status granted to an applicant who meets the prescribed entrance requirements of the institution.

Admission Tests – Also known as "college entrance exams," these tests are designed to provide a measure of a student's academic skills and help institutions evaluate how ready students are to do college-level work. The ACT® and the SAT® are two popular standardized admission tests used in the United States.

Advanced Standing Credit - Credit hours that an institution accepts toward a degree from courses that the student has earned elsewhere. Such credit may be given for work completed at another higher education institution, by examination i.e., "testing out," or by documented training during military service.

Application - Application is the process by which a prospective student submits the required forms and credentials to his/her chosen institution.

Associate's Degree - The Associate Degree is granted upon completion of a program of at least two, but less than four years of college work. The Associate Degree requires completion of a minimum of 60 credit hours.

Associate of Applied Science Degree - This degree is conferred upon students who have successfully completed a program of study designed to lead the individual directly into employment in a specific career. Applied Science degrees have the same requirements as those for the Associate Degree.

Bachelor's Degree - The undergraduate degree offered by four-year colleges and universities. The minimum credit hour requirement for a Bachelor's Degree is 120 hours.

CLEP® - The College Level Examination Program can be taken by students who want to obtain college credit by taking a proficiency test in selected courses. If the student scores high enough on the test, college credit can be awarded. There is a charge for each test taken.

College - A college is an institution of higher education that grants degrees and certificates. The term is also used to designate the organizational units of a university such as the College of Science or the College of Humanities.

College Application Essay - An essay that a college requires students to write and submit as part of their application. Some colleges require applicants to answer specific questions, while other institutions simply ask applicants to write about themselves. Colleges may refer to this as a "personal statement."

Convocation - An assembly of people, in this case at a college or university for a ceremony that begins official start of a college education.

Commencement: Graduation Ceremony.

Common Application - A standard application form accepted by all colleges that are members of the Common Application Association. You can fill out this application once and submit it to any one, or several, of any of the colleges that accept it.

Community College - A community college is a two-year institution of higher education.

Counselor - This person will help you select the correct courses, review the course requirements in the field you have selected to pursue and help you with any academic problems you may encounter.

Credit Hours - Courses taken in college are measured in credit hours. To earn one credit hour, a student must attend a class for one hour per week for the whole semester (usually 16 weeks). Classes are offered in 1 - 5 credit hour increments, and in rare cases, sometimes larger amounts.

Degree Requirements - Those requirements prescribed by institutions for completion of a program of study. Requirements may include a minimum number of hours, required GPA, prerequisite and elective courses within the specified major, and/or minor areas of study.

Degrees - Degrees are rewards for the successful completion of a prescribed program of study.

Elective - A class you can take that is not specifically required by your major or minor. A class you take for fun.

Estimated Family Contribution (EFC) – the amount of money you and your family will be expected to pay irrespective of where you go to school. The EFC is calculated by the Federal Government using information supplied on your Free Application for Federal Student Aid (FAFSA®).

Enrollment - The procedure by which students choose classes each semester, which also includes the assessment and collection of fees.

FAFSA® - Free Application for Federal Student Aid. This is *the* application for financial aid, including scholarships, loans, grants, college work-study and other federal and state programs.

Fees - Fees are additional charges over and above tuition. Fees may be charged to cover the cost of materials and equipment needed in certain courses, and they may be assessed for student events, programs, as well as publications.

Financial Aid – money made available to students from grants, scholarships, loans, and part-time employment (work-study) from federal, state, institutional, and private sources.

Full-Time Enrollment - A full-time student is enrolled in 12 or more credit hours in a semester (full-time status for a summer term is usually 6 credit hours).

Humanities Courses - Humanities courses are classes in subjects such as literature, philosophy, and the fine arts. Most undergraduate degrees require a certain number of humanities courses.

Junior College - A junior college is a two-year institution of higher education.

Grade Point Average (GPA) – Generally, the number obtained by dividing the total number of grade points earned as a result of a grade by the total number of credits attempted.

Major - A student's chosen field of study. It requires the successful completion of a specified number of credit hours/classes within a specified subject area.

Minor - A specific number of credit hours in a secondary field of study. It requires a specified number of credit hours/classes in this secondary field, usually 18, but this can vary from institution to institution.

Non-Credit Courses - These are classes or courses that do not meet the requirements for a certificate of a degree at an institution. Non-credit courses may are taken for a variety of reasons providing students with the opportunity to explore new fields of study, increase proficiency in a particular area, explore interests, or to enrich life experiences.

Open-Door Institution - Open-door institutions are generally public two-year junior or community colleges. The term "open-door" refers to an admission policy that basically allows anyone who is 18 years of age or older, whether or not a high school graduate, to be admitted to that college. Admission is contingent that they meet the requirements such as a specific ACT® or SAT® score, GED®, TASK®, or other assessment.

Part-Time Enrollment - A part-time student is enrolled in less than 12 credit hours in a semester (less than 6 during a summer term).

Placement Tests - Tests that measure the academic skills needed for college-level work. They cover reading, writing, math and sometimes other subjects. Placement test results help determine what courses you are academically prepared to take and whether you would benefit from developmental or skill enhancement classes.

Pre-enrollment - The method by which students select courses in advance of the official enrollment date.

Pre-requisite Courses - A course taken in preparation for another course. For example, Accounting 101 is needed to prepare for Accounting 201. In this case, Accounting 101 would be the prerequisite course.

Private Institutions - Private institutions rely on income from private donations, or from religious or other organizations, as well as student tuition. Private institutions are governed by a board of trustees.

Public Institutions - Public institutions receive funding, or partial funding, from the state or other governmental entities and are administered by public boards.

Registrar - The registrar of an institution is responsible for the maintenance of all academic records and may include such duties as maintaining class enrollments, providing statistical information on student enrollment, certification of athletic eligibility, student eligibility for honor rolls, certification of the eligibility of veterans, administering probation and retention policies and verification of the completion of degree requirements for graduation.

Resident - A student who lives in and meets the citizenship requirements for the state where a college or university is located. Tuition at public colleges and universities is often is less expensive for residents.

SAT® - These letters are acronyms for the American College Test This assessment is designed to measure a student's level of knowledge in basic areas such as math, science, English and social studies. Colleges may require the results of either the ACT® or SAT® before granting admission.

Schedule of Classes- A class schedule is a list of classes a student is taking, which includes course name, course number, the time and location of the class, and possibly the instructor.

Student Aid Report (SAR) – The report that you get back from the Federal Government that contains your Estimated Family Contribution (EFC).

Transcript - The transcript is a permanent academic record of a student. It may show courses taken, grades received, academic status and honors received, placement test scores, and so on.

Transfer of Credits - Some students attend more than one institution during their college career. When they move or transfer from one college to another, they also transfer accumulated credit hours from the former institution to the new one. The new institution determines which courses will apply toward graduation requirements.

Tuition - Tuition is the amount paid for each credit hour of enrollment at an institution. Tuition does not include the cost of books, fees, or room and board. Tuition charges vary from college to college and depends on factors such as if a student has resident or out-of-state status, and other variables such as whether the institution is publicly or privately financed.

Undergraduate - A student who is pursuing either a one, two, or four year degree.

University - A university is composed of undergraduate, graduate, and professional colleges and offers degrees in each.

Waiting List - The list of applicants who may be admitted to a college, or a class, if space becomes available.

Weighted Grade Point Average (GPA) - A grade point average that's calculated using a system that assigns a higher point value to grades in more difficult classes. For example, some high schools assign the value of 5.0 (instead of the standard 4.0) for an A earned in an AP or a dual credit class.

Sources:

DiGangi, C. (2015, February 27). Should You Take Out More Student Loan Money Than You Need? | Fox Business. Retrieved from http://www.foxbusiness.com/personal-finance/2015/02/27/should-take-out-more-student-loan-money-than-need/
Earnings and unemployment rates by educational attainment. (2015, April 2). Retrieved from http://www.bls.gov/emp/ep_chart_001.htm

Giang, V. (2013, July 16). What Young People Should Know Before Going To College - Business Insider. Retrieved from http://www.businessinsider.com/what-young-people-should-know-before-going-to-college-2013-7

Glenn, W. (2015, May 13). Everything You Need to Do the Summer Before College: A Checklist. Retrieved fromhttp://lifehacker.com/everything-you-need-to-do-the-summer-before-college-a-1704012158

FAFSA® on the Web - Federal Student Aid. (2015, May 10). Retrieved from https://fafsa.ed.gov/

Jeffers, S. J. (2007). *Feel the fear-- and do it anyway*. New York: Ballantine Books.

National Letter of Intent Home Page. (n.d.). Retrieved from http://www.nationalletter.org/

Preparing for College: Senior Checklist. (n.d.). Retrieved from http://www.nacacnet.org/studentinfo/articl es/Pages/Preparing-for-College-Senior-Checklist.aspx

Reed, D. (2010). *Living In The Now: A Guide To Living A More Fulfilled Life*. Glenville, WV: Darcon Publishing.

Wilson, P. (n.d.). 5 Strategies to Pay for College Today | Military.com. Retrieved from http://www.military.com/money/personal-finance/banking-and-savings/5-strategies-to-pay-for-college.html

ABOUT THE AUTHOR

Daniel A. Reed is an author, educator, speaker, as well as a full time high school counselor, who has worked with a multitude of students across the entire educational spectrum. He has taught classes at both the undergraduate and graduate level in general psychology, lifespan development, abnormal psychology, death and dying, counseling, human sexuality, theory of personality, and education, as well as co-created introduction to college life courses for two different institutions of higher education. In his current position he works with high school seniors who are getting ready to graduate and enter the "real world" after graduation, and has helped students collectively secure hundreds of thousands of dollars in scholarship and grant money.

Drawing on his experiences working in community mental health as a therapist, Daniel wrote, *Living in the NOW: A Guide to Living a More Fulfilled Life*, which focuses on helping people to relax and enjoy life more fully. He also has a blog, *Senior-itis* which is a resource for students and their parents to learn more and discuss issues related to the final year of school.

Follow Daniel on the web:

Website: www.DanielAReed.com
Twitter: @ProfessorDReed
Email: Daniel@DanielAReed.com
http://seniorinmysenioryear.blogspot.com/